CHALLENGING CRIME

A Portrait of the Cambridge Institute of Criminology

Editor: Catharine Walston
Advisory Editors: Anthony Bottoms, Manuel Eisner and Friedrich Lösel

MPhil students 2004–5 outside the Institute.

First published in 2009 by
Third Millennium Publishing Limited,
a subsidiary of Third Millennium Information Limited.

2–5 Benjamin Street
London
United Kingdom
EC1M 5QL
www.tmiltd.com

ISBN 978 1 906507 08 4

Edited by Catharine Walston
Designed by Susan Pugsley
Production by Bonnie Murray
Reprographics by Studio Fasoli, Italy
Printed by Printer Trento, Italy

Photo acknowledgements

The editors would like to thank the following for their assistance with illustrations: Karen Bates (Allies and Morrison); Wayne Boucher; Lucinda Bowditch; Catherine Byfield; Kim Campbell (Julie Spence's office); Adicea Castillo; Michael Derringer (photos on pp. 60, 71, 74, 76, 88, 105); Loraine Gelsthorpe; Dennis Gil (Allies and Morrison); Christina Goodwin (Paul Wiles's office); Mary Gower (Radzinowicz Librarian); Mick Hallett (PRC Wandsworth photos); Paul Heartfield (Paul Wiles's photographer); JET Photographic; Birthe Jorgensen; Martin Langenhorst (photo of Professor Albrecht on p. 121); Michael Marsland (Yale University Bulletin); Sarah Newsom (Wolfson Foundation); Denis Pannett; Sir Cam (photos on pp. 8, 14, 18, 21, 23, 41, 64, 98, 104, 122); Jonathan Smith (Archivist, Trinity College); David Thomas; Christelle Vorster (Warren Young's office); Linda Wills (Peterborough Tourist Information Centre); Naomi Young.

Although every reasonable effort has been made to identify copyright holders of images used in this book, any further information will be welcomed by the publishers.

The Institute is grateful for financial support for this publication from the Wakefield Trust.

Endpapers: Detail of tiled floor in the entrance to 7 West Road.

THIRD MILLENNIUM
PUBLISHING, LONDON

Contents

Foreword

In 2009 the University of Cambridge celebrates its 800th anniversary – a year in which we look back on great achievements as an international leader in teaching and research, and also reflect on current challenges and strategies for the future. I am very pleased to note that the Institute of Criminology takes a similar opportunity with its 50th anniversary, which falls in this same year. Of course, compared to the University as a whole, Criminology is still young. However, in a human life span, 50 years is more than long enough to enable parents to make a sound judgement on how their offspring have developed – and Cambridge looks with pride on its now adult child. As this book shows, the Institute's birth was no simple matter, and nor was it a matter of course that Cambridge – a small town with a relatively low crime rate – and not London, became its home. Fifty years later it is obvious that this was the right environment in which to nurture the newborn, and we are grateful to Sir Leon Radzinowicz and to the then Home Secretary Lord Butler for their initiative. In particular, the Wolfson Foundation deserves great thanks for its generous endowment which enabled the establishment of the Professorship and the Institute of Criminology.

Thanks to the engagement of its Directors and staff, the first Institute of Criminology in the United Kingdom grew into a world leader in its field. It is also well integrated into the Faculty of Law, the School of the Humanities and Social Sciences and the University as a whole. It has flourishing programmes for Master's and Doctoral students and makes important contributions to the Joint Schools Graduate Training Course and to undergraduate teaching in the Faculty of Law and the Faculty of Politics, Psychology, Sociology and International Studies. The Institute

is a pioneer in its part-time Diploma and MSt Programmes for senior practitioners, an area which becomes more and more important as the professions draw systematically on life-long learning. The Institute is also successful in its research activities, gaining external – indeed, international – recognition.

I congratulate the Institute on what has been achieved over the last 50 years and I wish it all the best for the future. This commemorative book not only provides information on the Institute's history, but will also entertain its readership and refresh good memories of our alumni – memories of both the 50 year-old criminological child and its 800 year-old mother, the University of Cambridge.

Professor Alison Richard
Vice-Chancellor of The University of Cambridge

Introduction

In 2001 I spent a few months as a Visiting Fellow at the Cambridge Institute of Criminology. At that time I didn't expect to be Director of the Institute when it celebrated its 50th anniversary in 2009 in conjunction with the 800th anniversary of the University. At the time of my visit it was a relatively cold early spring with snow around Easter. My office in the Institute was a small, poorly heated room in the back of 7 West Road facing the very impressive glass façade of the new Law Faculty building in the distance. I sat on a simple wooden chair, used my laptop on an old scratched desk, and the inkjet printer worked somewhat erratically. When I left the building in the evening I had to be careful not to trigger the security alarm system as I did once. I felt less guilty when I learnt that Tony Bottoms, who had been a regular in the building for many years, had similar problems with the alarm system.

In spite of these minor hassles, I enjoyed my stay at the Institute very much. I was warmly welcomed, had good conversations with staff members and other Visiting Fellows, and found time to finish some articles. However, most important for my very positive feelings were experiences that I would call 'spiritual', although this is a difficult term for an empirical researcher who admires Popper's critical rationalism. First was the scholarly spirit of the old University with its tradition as a world leader in research and higher education. And secondly, there was the specific spirit in the Institute of Criminology which had also achieved a world-wide reputation in its field. Both factors led me not to hesitate when I was asked some years later whether I would be interested in applying for the vacant Director's post.

A part of the spirit of Cambridge University derives from the beautiful old town with its ancient college buildings. It can easily be felt on a walk from the Institute through the Backs and King's College to the Old Schools. However, this tourist image of Cambridge cannot be separated from its spirit of scholarship and academic life: giants in science like Newton, a large number of Nobel Prize winners, leading positions in all recent university rankings, the international mix of students and academics, a strong dedication to the highest academic standards, intensive student supervision and care, mutual esteem for both individual and group achievement across all disciplines, a wide range of enjoyable and inspiring college activities, sensible democratic processes at most levels of decision making, and – behind everything – the clear and sometimes difficult aim to balance 800 years of a great tradition with the demands of a fast-changing modern world.

Although the Institute of Criminology is 750 years younger, its history and current activities reflect the basic characteristics of the University. Of course, there are no Nobel Prizes for achievements in criminology, yet academics from the Institute have probably been awarded more distinguished awards in their field than any other criminological department in the world. Within the Cambridge family of disciplines, some aspects of the Institute's profile are particularly worth mentioning.

Opposite: The new building, in the heart of the Sidgwick Site, was opened in 2005. For alumni of previous decades, memories of the Institute will be linked to 7 West Road, 150m away towards the University Library.

Below: Professor Friedrich Lösel, Director of the Institute of Criminology.

First is the Institute's interdisciplinary orientation, which was one of the main aims of its founding Director, Sir Leon Radzinowicz. Since Cesare Beccaria and the early days of criminology in the 18th century, it has always been a matter of debate whether crime should be investigated primarily within the most relevant disciplines (eg biology, economics, history, law, medicine, political science, psychology, sociology) or should be addressed in a more integrated discipline of criminology. As Sir Leon mentions in his *Adventures in Criminology*, there was some hesitation in bringing various disciplines together under the roof of the Cambridge Institute of Criminology. However, the following chapters of this book clearly demonstrate that integration was the right decision. Criminology as a standalone discipline has flourished and is one of the few areas to which the often-emphasised inter- or at least trans-disciplinary approach has been paid more than lip-service. Of course, all academics in our Institute have specific competences in their background disciplines, but they widened their views and learned about other perspectives via daily collaboration. Some visitors even ask about the background of a colleague because it is no longer obvious whether he/she came from criminal justice, psychology, sociology, or another discipline.

A second part of the Institute's profile is its strong international orientation which is, however, well balanced with its national activities. Whereas on average approximately 40 per cent of the University's graduate students come from overseas, the Institute's MPhil and PhD programmes attract nearly 60 per cent from other countries. The Institute's composition of academic staff is also international. Half of the established academic posts and many colleagues on fixed-term contracts are not British. Numerous Visiting Scholars and Fellows also contribute to the international orientation of our Institute. This orientation was part of Sir Leon's original mission for the Institute and developed more or less naturally over the years. It keeps the Institute sensitive to cultural issues, leads to broader perspectives in research and teaching, and supports transnational networks. However, this does, of course, not imply that the national issues of penal law and the justice system get less attention. Criminology's genuine relation to the legal framework inevitably requires studying not only general issues but also local and national problems of crime and its prevention.

This is reflected in a third characteristic of the Institute, namely its dedication to both basic and applied research. When in 1959 the then Home Secretary Rab Butler supported the foundation of the first British Institute of Criminology at Cambridge, it was the clear mission that this institution should undertake research that would contribute to an evidence-based crime policy. Although the Institute was always engaged in basic research, it was equally – some so-called critical criminologists may even say too much – devoted to applied research that could be used in practice and policy making. This orientation should not be seen as the combination of alternatives but as the dedication to a broad range of research types between two poles. On the one hand, there is nothing as practical as a good theory (Kurt Lewin). On the other hand, practical predictions and interventions are often the most rigorous empirical tests of theories. The Institute's balance between basic and applied research is indicated by numerous studies on delinquent development, situation- and person-oriented crime prevention, community factors and crime, sentencing, imprisonment, probation and offender rehabilitation. It is also clearly reflected in its current Research Centres on Prison Research, Penal Theory and Penal Ethics, Social Contexts of Pathways in Crime, and Experimental Criminology.

The following chapters of this book will describe these and many other activities of the Institute over 50 years of challenging crime. In both an informative and entertaining style, the book

Sir Leon Radzinowicz, founder of the Institute, from a portrait drawing of 1967.

presents the Institute's foundation and organisational development, staff members, various teaching programmes, research centres and projects, alumni, visitors, library, new building, and – last but not least – its generous donors and supporters. The journey through 50 years of research and teaching on the origins, prevention and control of crime will show why and how the Institute became a world leader in its field, whose contributions help to chart how society balances the need for social order with individual freedom under the rule of law. At a time when problems such as youth violence, terrorism, prison overcrowding and fear of crime are key issues in many countries – although crime figures are often decreasing – the work of the Institute is as relevant as ever.

Although the focus of the book is on the past, it will naturally lead to reflections about potential future developments. As criminologists often deal with predictions (eg on recidivism or crime rates), they know the pitfalls of this business. We do well to remember the former Peterhouse Fellow and famous 19th-century physicist William Thomson, who became Professor at Glasgow and was honoured as Lord Kelvin. In spite of his outstanding scholarship, he forecast no future for the radio and the impossibility of flying machines which are heavier than air or of x-rays which he saw as a joke. Predicting the future of an Institute that deals with crime in a highly dynamic world may bear similar risks of error. For example, who would have anticipated at the beginning of the 21st century that suicide aircraft terrorists would destroy the World Trade Center in New York or that pirates in rubber-boats could capture super-tankers? Therefore, I will only briefly sketch a few potential perspectives to which the Institute can contribute by its activities.

Although the (also badly predicted) current financial and economic crisis has led to budget cuts in the academic world and increased monetary problems for Cambridge University, the Institute seems to cope relatively well. In spite of its small number of only eight established academic posts, the Institute has substantially increased its research income and currently employs almost 60 people. The number of PhD students is at an all-time high, our MPhil courses are well subscribed and – after a difficult transition from direct Home Office funding to the world-wide open market – we see a strong increase in students on our Applied Criminology programmes for senior practitioners from the Police, Prisons and Probation Services. In a globalised world, crime and its prevention become more and more an international issue and there is increasing demand for criminological research and teaching in Asia, South America, Africa and other parts of the world. Because of its international orientation and long expertise in practice-oriented studies, the Institute can become an important agent in this development.

Current scholars of the Institute have carried out numerous evaluation studies and systematic reviews on the effects of crime prevention measures, for example, on closed circuit television, improved street lighting, hot spots policing, cognitive-behavioural rehabilitation programmes, treatment of sexual offenders, different types of prison regimes, public versus private prison organisation, restorative justice, child- and family-oriented crime prevention, programmes for juvenile delinquents, parenting orders, programmes against school bullying and so forth. Various staff members play a key role in the development of the Campbell Crime and Justice Collaboration, a world-wide network which promotes the best evidence on measures of crime prevention and control. It follows the model of the Cochrane Collaboration whose reviews are now the state-of-the-art knowledge base in medicine. In collaboration with the Campbell Crime and Justice Group, the National Police Improvement Agency (NPIA), the Ministry of Justice and other institutions, Cambridge Criminology works on the mission of assisting in the formulation of evidence-based crime policy. Our Applied Criminology teaching programmes offer an ideal framework for the establishment of a network of experts who can transfer this approach to their local sphere of influence. In the longer run, these activities may contribute to the development of a larger centre that follows the model of the National Institute for Health and Clinical Excellence (NIHCE).

Another perspective relates to the Institute's particular strength in longitudinal research. The Cambridge Study in Delinquent Development, which has been running for more than 40 years, has provided ground-breaking knowledge on the origins, risk factors, and protective factors for the onset and aggravation of, or desistance from, criminal behaviour. The more recent Sheffield Study, Peterborough Study, Zurich Study and Erlangen-Nuremberg Study started at different ages (ranging from young adulthood to preschool age) and have now been already running between seven and ten years. This unique set of prospective longitudinal studies will show how far findings from the Cambridge Study can be generalised across countries and today's world with increased migration and other social and material changes.

The Institute can use its broad disciplinary range to intensify the links between criminology and relevant areas of recent brain research. Of course, the Institute should not follow simple pendulum swings between social science and bioscience explanations of crime. In contrast,

Panoramic view of Cambridge looking towards the University Library from the Sidgwick Site.

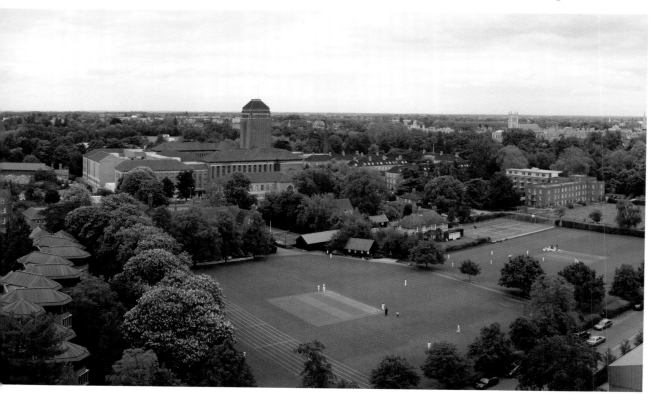

research shows important interactions between the social, psychological and biological factors of influence. In the longer term, such studies may not only lead to more individualised programmes of prevention and rehabilitation but also more differentiated concepts of criminal responsibility and sentencing. Many studies in the currently flourishing neurobiological domain are only cross-sectional and based on small samples. The Cambridge Institute with its interdisciplinary and longitudinal orientation is an ideal place for more long-term and integrated approaches instead of unfruitful polarisation between criminological paradigms. Again, this perspective would be fully in accordance with Sir Leon's vision of criminology as a bio-psycho-social discipline.

All directors over the last 50 years have had their own vision of the Institute's best development. However, all of them also adapted sensitively to the reality, to opportunities as well as the serious financial constraints of higher education in Britain. Therefore, I will leave speculation about our great potential for the future and return to the solid ground of the past. This leads me finally to the most recent activity of the Institute: the production of this book. When I brought this idea to our Academic Staff Committee there was great enthusiasm and we immediately established a 50th anniversary committee. This committee worked very effectively and over time we made a collective effort to achieve what is now in front of you. This leaves me with the pleasant duty of thanking my colleagues and other collaborators. My greatest thanks go to Sir Anthony Bottoms who, although recently retired and not at all obliged to, invested an immense amount of time and energy to present the correct facts in this volume. I am also very grateful to Catharine Walston, who was a very competent and sensitive editor whose polite reaction to numerous changes reminded me of the ancient Greek stoics. Manuel Eisner helped a lot in the final phase of editing for which I would like to say 'Danke, Manuel'. Of course, Catharine, Tony, Manuel and I realised that it would be almost impossible to produce a manageable-sized history and current record of the Institute that included everything worthy of note. We aimed, therefore, for an appropriate balance and ask for a measure of understanding and indulgence.

Many colleagues from the Institute wrote, edited or collaborated on chapters and we decided at an early stage not to attribute individual authorship. We leave it to the detective competence of the reader to find out who wrote what, which in the case of particular studies and research centres will not be too taxing. Although we are proud of the collective effort by the entire Institute, I am particularly grateful to my colleagues Tony Bottoms, Manuel Eisner, David Farrington, Loraine Gelsthorpe, Mary Gower, Adrian Grounds, Andrew von Hirsch, Roy King, Alison Liebling, Larry Sherman, Stuart Stone and Per-Olof Wikström. In addition, I wish to thank the Lord Chief Justice, Sir Igor Judge, who contributed a vignette on David Thomas. Many thanks also to our colleague from the Law Faculty, Nicky Padfield, and other former members of the Institute and international friends who helped by contributing their memories, photos and documents. Jenny Lovell and Nicholas Champkins of Allies and Morrison architects were extremely kind in writing descriptions of the creative process involved in designing our new building. Behind every publication of this type, there is always an enormous organisational, technical and creative effort. For this I wish to thank Caroline Edwards, Naomi Young and Catherine Byfield from the Institute and Chris Fagg and Susan Pugsley from Third Millennium Publishers. Last but not least, I am very grateful to our Vice-Chancellor, Professor Alison Richard for writing a foreword for our volume. It shows that the 800 year-old mother looks with satisfaction on its 50 year-old child. As an Institute with a strong profile in developmental criminology we hope that our research contributes to a society in which children are similarly valued in all families.

Chapter 1

A 750-year-old Mother Adopts a New Child: The Institute of Criminology 1959–2009

The University of Cambridge traces its foundation to some specific events in the year 1209. It was a time of struggle for power between the Pope and King John, with the Pope having issued an interdict on England in 1208. Within this general context, a local incident at Oxford led to some remarkable consequences, as Damien Leader (1988) explains in the first volume of the official history of Cambridge University. A scholar at Oxford University killed a townswoman with an arrow. The mayor of Oxford and his helpers were unable to apprehend the perpetrator, so instead they seized two or three of his housemates, and had them hanged, with the consent of King John. According to the laws then in force, the defendants, being like all university students in minor church orders, should have been arraigned before a church court - and had this happened, they would have escaped the gallows. It was, as Leader (1988, p.17) puts it, a 'clear violation of the privilege of clerics' - and, of course, it was a violation exercised on this occasion against persons other than the perpetrator. So, Leader continues, 'the scholars of Oxford ran for their lives', and the University went into voluntary suspension, as other European universities had done before 'when local authorities infringed upon their privileges'. On this occasion, most of Oxford's scholars left the city – some to Paris (Leedham-Green 1996, p.3) and some temporarily to Reading, while others trekked eastwards, eventually settling in Cambridge to found their own seat of learning there. Thus, it has been wryly said that Cambridge alumni 'might find it slightly embarrassing to admit that [their *alma mater*] possibly owes its origins to the murder of a prostitute by an Oxford student' (quoted in Leader 1988, p.17). More pertinently for present purposes, if criminology is, as is frequently stated, 'the study of crime and its causes, and of social responses to crime' then, without question, the foundation of Cambridge University is a topic with a significantly criminological dimension.

Given these intriguing origins, it is perhaps fitting that Cambridge in the 20th century became the first university in the United Kingdom to establish an Institute of Criminology. The way in which this happened, however, was complex.

In the late 1930s, a very able Polish criminologist, who had been trained in Paris, Geneva and Rome, made a visit to England to study developments in penal policy. This scholar, Leon Radzinowicz, had for some time been concerned about political developments in Poland, and, although he had originally intended to return after his English visit, circumstances dictated that he should remain in the UK. Through his contacts with the Howard League for Penal Reform, he was introduced to a law don at Trinity Hall, Cambridge, J.W. Cecil Turner. Turner can be regarded as the unsung hero of the development of criminology in Cambridge. In the 1930s, criminal law was often described as the Cinderella subject of academic legal studies - and it was once remarked, extending this metaphor, that on the same basis criminology was Cinderella's illegitimate daughter. Cecil Turner, very unusually for his time, not only regarded criminal law as a subject worthy of serious academic attention, he was also actively interested in penal reform. By 1940, Turner had already persuaded the University's Faculty Board of Law to establish a

Trinity College. Trinity was Leon Radzinowicz's college and also the college where Rab Butler became Master on his retirement from Parliament.

An engraving (c.1851) showing the Senate House (right) and the Old Schools (left) where the Institute's first year's teaching took place.

'Committee to Consider the Promotion of Research and Teaching in Criminal Science'. In the following year (December 1941) the University formally approved the foundation of a tiny 'Department of Criminal Science' within the Faculty of Law, led jointly by Turner and Radzinowicz.

Leon Radzinowicz set to work on his own personal *magnum opus*, his five-volume *History of English Criminal Law* (1948–86), a magnificent and very carefully researched work of legal-historical scholarship, detailing the development of criminal justice since 1750 in his adopted country. But, even in this early period, Cambridge criminology was not confined to Radzinowicz's personal scholarship and Turner's legal work. In the 1950s, the Department of Criminal Science also began to carry out a few empirical research studies, and for these the work of a young recruit from the London School of Economics, F.H. ('Derick') McClintock, was of pivotal importance. Yet, as Radzinowicz himself would subsequently affirm, this early work – while undeniably important as a beginning – did not amount to the full-scale adoption of criminology as a subject by the University.

Everything changed in the late 1950s. The Howard League, led on this occasion by the remarkable Margery Fry, decided to press upon the government the case for the establishment of a fully-fledged and nationally prominent Institute of Criminology. The League argued, with justification, that the United Kingdom lagged well behind many other countries in the development of criminology as an academic subject, and that the time had come to remedy the situation. A formal letter to this effect was sent in June 1957 by the Secretary of the League to the then Home Secretary, R.A. ('Rab') Butler. In the following month, Margery Fry discussed the matter with Butler, whose response was favourable. Hence, in March 1958, Butler sent official letters to the Vice-Chancellors of the University of London and the University of Cambridge, saying:

it seems to me that a stage has been reached when the establishment of an institute of criminology under the aegis of one of the universities would be of great value, in order to give a new impulse to studies in this field, to set high standards in a subject whose academic status is not yet universally recognised, and to give direction to efforts which have so far been largely uncoordinated. As I see it, such an institute, which would no doubt have to draw its staff from several faculties concerned with different aspects of the subject, would have three main functions: to promote research, to train post-graduate teachers of criminology, and to consider how best to develop the teaching of

'Rab' Butler (1902–82). After lobbying by the Howard League, Richard Austen Butler, then Home Secretary under Harold Macmillan, initiated the establishment of a nationally prominent institute of criminology in 1958. Reproduced by permission of the Master and Fellows of Trinity College.

J.W. Cecil Turner (1886–1968), Fellow of Trinity Hall and editor of Kenny's Outlines of Criminal Law *and of* Russell on Crime, *the unsung hero of the development of criminology in Cambridge, responsible for facilitating Radzinowicz's move to Cambridge.*

criminology both for non-graduates in the universities and for those outside the universities (such as magistrates, police, members of the prison service and probation officers) who are concerned with the administration of justice and the prevention of crime. These are all functions for which there is a growing need that ought to be met.

(Radzinowicz 1988, p.133)

It can therefore truly be said that the Institute of Criminology 'owes its birth to the initiative of R.A. Butler, an outstanding Home Secretary' (Radzinowicz 1988, p.v).

But where would such an Institute be located? Those at the Howard League who had promoted the concept of an Institute had always assumed that such a body would be based in London, which was after all both the nation's capital and a major metropolis with a significant crime problem. Moreover, London University had developed the then-nascent social sciences (especially at the London School of Economics [LSE]) to a much greater extent than had most British universities at the time, and had welcomed the émigré German criminologist Hermann Mannheim to the LSE as a Reader in Criminology. Cambridge, by contrast, was a medium-sized town with little crime, and in the University the social sciences (other than economics) were notably underdeveloped. Margery Fry's 'personal view', confided to the Home Secretary, was that 'the present teaching of criminology at Cambridge was too closely linked to the teaching of criminal law and that there would be a danger of this legal influence continuing to predominate' if the proposed Institute were located in Cambridge (quoted in Radzinowicz 1988, p.8).

Despite this background, London University's formal response to the Home Secretary's 1958 letter was decidedly lukewarm, while the response from Cambridge was positive. So the Home Office's choice was made, more or less by default, in favour of Cambridge. There was still a significant financial problem, but that was solved by various means, most notably by an extremely generous special grant of £150,000 from the Wolfson Foundation, which included funds for the endowment of the first established Chair in Criminology in the United Kingdom. (Details of these matters may be found in Radzinowicz 1988, chs. 3–9.) So it came about that in 1959, the year of its 750th anniversary, the University of Cambridge formally approved two historic 'Graces' (resolutions): the first for the establishment of an Institute of Criminology (Grace 4 of 7 February 1959), and the second for the establishment of the Wolfson Professorship of Criminology, with Leon Radzinowicz as its first holder (Grace 1 of 31 October 1959).

Laying the Foundations: the Radzinowicz years

Leon Radzinowicz remained in post as the first Wolfson Professor of Criminology until 1973, and he was also appointed as the Director of the new Institute of Criminology. In these vital early years he laid some very firm foundations for the work of the Institute.

- **Interdisciplinarity**. Radzinowicz was convinced that full interdisciplinarity was a fundamental prerequisite of a flourishing Institute of Criminology. This was reflected in the choice of the three core teaching and research staff at the time of the Institute's foundation: they were Derick McClintock, with his training in sociology and economics (and who also provided continuity from the former Department of Criminal Science); John Martin, who had obtained a doctorate in social policy from LSE; and Donald West, a clinical psychiatrist. Interdisciplinarity has remained a key feature of the Institute throughout its history, although the balance of specific disciplines has varied from time to time.

7 West Road, the Institute's home for more than 40 years.

- **A suitable building**. The Wolfson Foundation stated formally and publicly that its foundation grant for the Institute 'was made on the understanding that suitable and permanent accommodation would be provided by the University' (Wolfson Foundation 1960, pp.16–17). The University, however, was initially unable to meet this requirement. Two interim steps were therefore taken: First, the Institute was granted use of some existing University premises, initially for a short time at No. 4 Scroope Terrace (1959–62) (now part of the Faculty of Architecture and Art History), and then from Easter 1962 at No. 7 West Road, part of the University's then-developing Sidgwick Site where a number of departments in the humanities and social sciences were being housed. No. 7 West Road was explicitly assigned to the Institute as 'temporary premises', but, as we shall see, this 'temporary' occupation was to last for over 40 years! Meanwhile, and secondly, in order to help meet the Institute's need for permanent accommodation, the University in 1960 decided to lay aside a portion (£40,000) of the Wolfson Foundation's total foundation grant, to form the nucleus of a Building Fund for the Institute.

- **Library**. From the outset, 'the creation of a Library was regarded as of the first importance by the Wolfson Foundation' (Radzinowicz 1988, p.104). Leon Radzinowicz, therefore, set about the daunting task of creating a world-class research library, starting from a set of empty shelves. He was greatly assisted by a special grant from the Ford Foundation, and by the enthusiasm and sterling work of the Institute's first two librarians, Joan Friedman (subsequently Senior Lecturer in Librarianship at Sheffield University) and Martin Wright (subsequently Director of the Howard League for Penal Reform). What emerged became, it is widely agreed, the best criminological library in the United Kingdom and one of the best in the world. That this was achieved in the special context of Cambridge University, where traditionally the libraries of individual departments are not regarded as research libraries, was remarkable. Very appropriately, on Leon Radzinowicz's retirement, the library was renamed in his honour as the 'Radzinowicz Library of Criminology'.

- **Location within the Faculty of Law**. Given Cambridge structures, the Institute needed to be located within a specific Faculty. The obvious solution was location within the Faculty of Law - partly because the Department of Criminal Science had been nurtured within the Law Faculty; and partly because there was at that date no Social Science Faculty to provide a possible alternative home. This structural relationship has remained the same throughout the half-century of the Institute's existence. The interests of the Institute and its larger partner are not always identical, but the relationship between the two bodies has in general been mutually supportive and helpful. It is fitting to record here that the Institute owes a special debt to a number of Chairmen of the Law Faculty who have, over the years, been real friends in times of need (see chapter 12).

• **Research**. Naturally, the Institute of Criminology was expected to pursue high-quality research. During Radzinowicz's Directorship, the expectation was that all staff research would be funded by the Home Office. Moreover, while each academic staff member was, of course, expected to initiate proposals for his/her own research, nevertheless 'no project would be taken up unless it was approved by the Director', and on one occasion a proposed project was vetoed (Radzinowicz 1988, pp.90, 97). As Roger Hood (2002, p.xxi) has noted, in matters such as this Radzinowicz's somewhat dirigiste Directorial style was akin to that of a 'continental Professor', and 'not what we have become used to these days'. Nevertheless, some remarkably good and useful research emerged from this regime. Most famously – and despite some initial Directorial doubts (see chapter 5) – soon after the Institute's foundation Donald West far-sightedly initiated what has become a landmark longitudinal research project on criminal careers, The Cambridge Study in Delinquent Development. This study, easily the most significant single piece of research to have been developed during the Institute's first half-century, is still ongoing. (Since 1982, it has been under the distinguished leadership of Professor David Farrington, who began working on the project in the late 1960s under Donald West). Other important research in these

The Institute's first home at 4 Scroope Terrace, now the main entrance to the Department of Art History. Photo by Wayne Boucher.

early years included Derick McClintock's work on patterns of recorded crime (McClintock 1963, McClintock and Avison 1968) and studies by John Martin on police deployment (Martin and Wilson 1969) and the social consequences of crime (Martin and Webster 1971).

• **One-year postgraduate course**. Although it had been recognised by the University as early as 1941, the Department of Criminal Science had never engaged in any regular teaching. Indeed, even nationally at that time students could rarely pursue criminology courses; there was only the occasional possibility of taking an optional course as part of a broader degree programme, such as a criminology paper in the LLM at the University of London. In October 1961, therefore, an historic moment was experienced as 18 postgraduate students from five continents assembled in Cambridge, to become collectively the members of the first-ever full-time postgraduate course in criminology in the United Kingdom. The Institute was still then in Scroope Terrace, which had no suitable lecture room; so rather symbolically the lectures and seminars were held in a room in the Old Schools, overlooking 'East Court', the small courtyard which contains 'the oldest university buildings at Cambridge…built c.1350–1400' (Rawle 1985, p.189). Those successfully completing the postgraduate course obtained a Diploma in Criminology, and they were to be the first of a regular succession of postgraduate student cohorts who have begun their criminological studies in Cambridge every year from 1961 to the present time. The Course Director for the first few years was John Martin, who deserves great credit for establishing the course on a very firm footing. (The postgraduate course is described in chapter 3, and some of its successful alumni in chapter 9).

• **Doctoral studies**. Doctoral studies began more slowly, but were always an integral part of the plan for the Institute. The first successful doctoral student was Roger Hood, who subsequently returned to join the academic staff of the Institute in 1967, when John Martin moved to a Chair at Southampton (see also chapter 9). Hood's doctoral thesis, on the history of the borstal system (Hood 1966) was published and became an influential book.

• **Undergraduate teaching**. Undergraduate teaching was also promoted, to a limited extent. This was done first by mounting an optional course in criminology within the undergraduate Law Tripos (Radzinowicz 1988, chs 22 and 23), and then – after Cambridge's somewhat belated acceptance of a Social and Political Sciences Tripos in the late 1960s – an optional course in that degree also. These courses have remained permanent and valuable elements of the total work of the Institute.

• **'Building Bridges with the Practical World'**. Butler's 1958 letter (noted above) had referred to an institute of criminology as potentially teaching 'those…who are concerned with the administration of justice and the prevention of crime'. From the outset, therefore, Leon Radzinowicz was concerned that the Institute should not only be a centre of academic excellence, but should also reach out to 'build bridges', as he put it, with the concerns of criminal justice practitioners. The first such venture, a short course which became known as the Senior Course in Criminology, took place in July 1960 – before the first postgraduate course. (Later developments in 'bridge-building' are described in chapter 3).

• **National Conferences in Criminology**. At the time of the Institute's foundation, there was no regular national forum where UK criminologists could meet and confer. It was thought to be appropriate for the country's first Institute of Criminology to act as a convenor for such occasions, so the first National Conference in Criminology was called by the Institute in 1964. Thereafter, conferences were held biennially until 1979, but – given the rapid spread of criminology to many more universities – they were then rightly superseded by what became the flourishing biennial and then annual conferences of the British Society of Criminology.

Leon Radzinowicz c.1950, founder of the Institute. Reproduced by permission of the Master and Fellows of Trinity College.

With the exception of the national conferences and the procedures for initiating research within the Institute, all the substantive aspects of the original vision for the Institute have been retained, though the 'bridges with the practical world' now have a different character (see chapter 3). The retention of so many of these original elements bears testimony to the soundness of the foundations that Leon

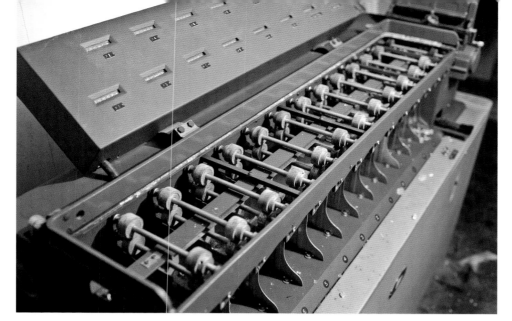

The sorter-counter machine, in the basement of 7 West Road. An invaluable tool in assisting with data processing before the computer age, the sorter-counter or tabulating machine worked by sorting data-punched cards into pockets and counting them.

Radzinowicz laid down. A quick scan of the matters set out above will also provide ample evidence of the huge energy and enthusiasm displayed by all members of the Institute's staff in these early years, in bringing such an ambitious programme to fruition.

Two episodes that occurred towards the end of Radzinowicz's tenure in different ways pointed towards the future.

The first occurred as a by-product of the final British debates on capital punishment. Parliament had voted to abolish that penalty in 1965, but only for a temporary five-year period. The late 1960s were a time of public concern about violence, so the Labour government in 1969 found itself wishing to make abolition permanent, but also needing to signal an understanding of public anxieties. During the Parliamentary debates leading to final abolition, it was therefore announced by the then Home Secretary (James Callaghan) that the Institute would be commissioned to undertake some special research studies relating to 'the growth of violent crime' (HCDeb.vol.793, cols.1159–60, 16 December 1969). The incident illustrates the Institute's closeness to the Home Office at this time, but the longer-term consequences are also interesting. The most important research to emerge from this special programme of work was that led by the late Richard F. Sparks, investigating the technical strengths and weaknesses of the so-called 'victim studies' that had then been recently pioneered in the United States (see Sparks, Genn and Dodd 1977). 'Victim studies' are surveys of the general population, asking respondents to report victimisations for criminal incidents, whether or not these have been reported to the police. Sparks' study, which focused on violent offences, was the first victim study to be completed in the UK, and became a vital forerunner to the eventual series of national 'British Crime Surveys' that have been commissioned by the Home Office since 1982. It was also one of the first pieces of research to uncover how frequent is the phenomenon that we now call 'repeat victimisation' (see Bottoms and Costello 2009). In these ways, like West's Cambridge Study, Sparks' research pointed towards the future in empirical criminology.

But another incident produced a challenge that was to be more theoretical and political. The archetypical year of student radicalism in both Europe and the United States is, of course, famously 1968. In a more minor key, that was also the year when a period of radical challenge in British criminology was initiated, as a small group of sociological criminologists 'met...fittingly enough in Cambridge in the middle of the Third National Conference of Research and Teaching in Criminology, organised by the Institute and opened by the Home Secretary' (Cohen 1981, p.233). This group subsequently formed the 'National Deviancy Symposium', which for a number of years met regularly at York, in conscious opposition to Cambridge's National Conferences. As the above quotation implies, they were critical of orthodox criminology, and they perceived the Institute to be far too closely linked to the Establishment through its strong ties to the Home Office. They also considered that too much of the Institute's research was 'positivistic' and designed to assist official policymaking. Some years later, Radzinowicz described the new movement (which, as time was to show, itself contained within it several different theoretical strands) as 'to some extent inevitable and to some extent misguided' (Radzinowicz 1988, p.115). He was probably right on both counts, but a fuller assessment would also have added that the radical critique was 'to some extent accurate and valuable'.

The Institute experienced some major changes of personnel in the early 1970s. Leon Radzinowicz resigned as Director in 1972, though he did not retire from the Wolfson Professorship until 1973. Derick McClintock steered the Institute skilfully through the transitional year 1972–3 as Acting Director, as he had in 1962–3 when Leon Radzinowicz was on sabbatical leave. In these and other ways, going back indeed to the pre-Institute days, Derick McClintock 'brought many fruitful benefits to criminology in Cambridge' (Radzinowicz 1998, p.162), and many former students also remember with gratitude his wise career advice. In 1974, however, he left Cambridge to become the first Professor of Criminology at Edinburgh University. The previous year, Dr Nigel Walker of Oxford was elected as the second Wolfson Professor of Criminology and Director of the Institute, and subsequently Roger Hood left the Institute to replace Walker as Reader in Criminology at Oxford. Thus within a couple of years, the small Institute staff lost three key figures: Leon Radzinowicz, Derick McClintock, and Roger Hood.

Consolidation, Liberalisation, and Broadening, 1973–84

Nigel Walker had been trained as an undergraduate in classics and philosophy. His initial career was as a civil servant in the Scottish Office, though he retained strong intellectual interests during this period, publishing books on the history of psychotherapy and on morale in the civil service. He had become Reader in Criminology at Oxford University in 1961, and had rapidly established a strong reputation there. In Cambridge, he took steps to modify Radzinowicz's

The first postgraduate course in Criminology, 1961–2

The first postgraduate course comprised seven lecture courses, namely 'Development of Criminological Thought' (Professor Leon Radzinowicz), 'Development of Penological Thought and Practice' (Sir Lionel Fox, though delivered by Professor Radzinowicz following Fox's death in October 1961), 'Psychiatric and Psychological Aspects of Criminal Conduct' (Dr Donald West, Dr Peter Scott and others), 'Sociology of Crime' (Professor D.R. Cressey, Dr T. Morris and others), 'Methods of Criminological Research' (Professor C. Moser, Dr J.P. Martin and others), 'Non-Institutional and Institutional Methods of Punishment and Treatment' (Mr F.H. McClintock, Miss J.F.S. King and others), and 'Enforcement of the Criminal Law' (various lecturers). Courses varied in length but some comprised up to 20 lectures and a similar number of seminars.

Interestingly, the course also included an important element of practical learning. A significant number of 'visits of observation' were arranged to, for example, Scotland Yard, a borstal, several prisons and the Home Office Research Unit. Additionally, students were expected to shadow the work of a probation officer for a week during the Christmas vacation, and to attend several sessions of the Magistrates' Courts.

View towards the University Library from the stair window of 7 West Road.

directorial style and to promote a more pluralistic Institute community (see Walker 2003); for example, the obligation to seek research funds only from the Home Office was abandoned.

Academically, Nigel Walker's wide interests in psychiatry, penal theory and reform, probation, and the history of crime and insanity facilitated the broadening of the Institute's criminological vision. His book *Punishment, Danger, and Stigma: The Morality of Criminal Justice* (1980) was a significant contribution to penal philosophy, a topic that has remained high on the Institute's agenda to the present time (see chapter 6). Also, Nigel Walker became interested in the subjective cognitive processes gone through by potential offenders before finally deciding whether to commit a crime. He obtained funds for a pioneering research study on this topic that was conducted by Trevor Bennett and Richard Wright (1984), both of whom went on to conduct further important research in this nascent field of 'offender decision-making'.

The 1970s were years of some turbulence in British criminology. Critical and Marxist scholarship was flowering, and there were early signs of a feminist and gender-conscious criminology. Fresh appointments brought (in one case indirectly) an element of both movements into the Institute. In 1973 Allison Morris, who later became a leading scholar internationally on restorative justice, replaced Derick McClintock. During her years in Cambridge she added significant publications in the liberal feminist tradition to her earlier work on juvenile justice. Shortly afterwards, Colin Sumner was appointed to a post in sociological criminology. Rooted in Marxism and 'The New Criminology', Sumner developed influential theoretical work on censure, and he also studied the effects of imperialist exploitation on crime in developing countries.

At the same time, other Institute staff members continued to pursue strands of research which in those years some 'new' criminologists would have perceived as 'old-fashioned'. More specifically, in 1973, 1977 and 1982 Donald West and David Farrington published what proved to be three very important reports on the adolescent and early adulthood phases of the Cambridge Study. Also, David Thomas's distinguished work on sentencing law (beginning with *Principles of Sentencing* 1970) became very prominent, and it added a further element to the broadening of scope of the Institute's research during this period.

Institutionally, these were years of consolidation and recognition. Although the University had formally adopted the Institute in 1959, there were still some in Cambridge who were sceptical of the viability and respectability of criminology as an academic subject. Gradually, these doubts dissipated. Important steps towards recognition were taken in the late 1970s, including perhaps most symbolically the re-designation of the one-year postgraduate course: from the academic year 1977–8, with no change of syllabus, the qualification obtained by successful students became a Master of Philosophy (MPhil) degree, instead of a Diploma in Criminology.

Nigel Walker had never intended to remain as Director until his retirement. In 1981, therefore, while retaining the Wolfson Chair he stood down as Director, handing the administrative reins to Donald West for three years. Then, in 1984, both retired from the University simultaneously, though happily both continued to live in Cambridge and to contribute to the life of the Institute.

Promoting Good Research and Practical Relevance 1984–99

In 1984 Anthony Bottoms became the third Wolfson Professor and the fourth Director of the Institute. He came from the University of Sheffield, where he had held a personal chair, but he was also the first alumnus to lead the Institute, having been a student on the Institute's first postgraduate course. During his 14 years as Director, Anthony Bottoms broadened and strengthened the Institute's role as one of the world's prime criminology departments. He successfully used the breadth of his own academic interests (see chapter 2) to promote a vibrant multidisciplinary research community.

As Director he sought 'to develop criminological knowledge in a spirit of free inquiry, with each staff member having the freedom to develop his or her research work in the way that seems to be most academically appropriate and rigorous' (Bottoms 1998). This 'spirit of free inquiry' saw a flourishing of new empirical research including, for example, important early studies on policing and crime prevention by Trevor Bennett, research on gender and the criminal justice system by Loraine Gelsthorpe, and a number of research projects on prisons.

Prison studies had not been among the foremost topics of interest for the Institute in its first quarter-century, but soon after his appointment as Director Anthony Bottoms was invited to become a member of a Home Office group advising on long-term prisons, and this led directly to a major research project that he directed on issues relating to the maintenance of order in maximum security prisons (Sparks, Bottoms and Hay 1996). Meanwhile, Alison Liebling also conducted important research on prison suicides, initially as a doctoral student and then in postdoctoral work; and this led naturally to further research, for example on incentives systems in prisons. The momentum thus created soon generated a strong prisons research group, led by Alison Liebling, which in due course became the Prisons Research Centre (see chapter 6).

Equally, Anthony Bottoms strengthened the Institute's reputation as a leading centre for research on penal theory, a research strand that had originally been introduced to the Institute by Nigel Walker. Under his directorship the Institute was fortunate to recruit, as Honorary Professor of Penal Theory and Penal Law, one of the foremost philosophers of punishment, Andrew von Hirsch. He currently leads the Research Centre on Penal Theory and Penal Ethics (see chapter 6). To give further recognition to this strand of work, the Institute in 1997 inaugurated an annual Nigel Walker Lecture, initially primarily focused on penal theory. This lecture rapidly became a pivotal scholarly event in the academic year, so that its scope has now been broadened to encompass criminology of all kinds.

In the 1990s, a leading Swedish criminologist, Per-Olof Wikström (see chapter 6), was recruited to the Institute after Colin Sumner's move to a chair at the University of East London. Wikström gained rapid promotion to a Cambridge chair, and he combined his intellectual interests in criminal

Staff and students on the first Diploma course, 1961–2. Cecil Turner is seated in the centre with Joan King to his right and Joan Friedman to his left. John Martin is seated next to Joan Friedman; Leon Radzinowicz stands behind her. Anthony Bottoms, a student on the course, is on the far right.

Diploma in Criminology awarded to Anthony Bottoms in 1962. This certificate now hangs in the Sir Anthony Bottoms Room on the first floor of the Institute.

careers and in ecological criminology to propose a major fresh longitudinal study with a strong ecological dimension. This study is based in Peterborough, an historic town recently greatly expanded as a London overspill destination; and generous funding for ten years has been obtained from the Economic and Social Research Council (ESRC) (see chapter 6).

Administratively, a major preoccupation for the Director of the Institute during these years concerned the Institute's accommodation. In a complex series of negotiations (outlined in chapter 11), it was often necessary to re-state the Wolfson Foundation's understanding that its foundation grant was made on the assumption that the University would provide a suitable permanent home for the Institute. Happily, in the late 1990s, there was a formal Review of the Institute by the University's General Board, which gave strong support to the Institute's aspirations, and urged speedy action. Thus, by the time that Anthony Bottoms stepped down as Director, it was clear that this problem would soon be solved, although exactly how remained to be addressed.

An important teaching innovation occurred in these years in relation to PhD students. Traditionally, in Cambridge as in most British universities, completing a PhD was a rather solitary business, very much focused on the supervisor-supervisee relationship, and containing no formal teaching inputs. In the Institute as elsewhere, this began to change in the late 1980s, and the process accelerated in the 1990s. The stimulus to change was twofold. First, the PhD students themselves expressed a wish for more group meetings, so that they could learn from each other's experiences and discuss them with a senior member of staff. Secondly, there was external pressure from the ESRC, which wanted additional methodological training to become a standard part of the doctoral experience; hence, a successful doctoral candidate would acquire a broader range of methodological skills than those strictly required by the substance of his/her dissertation. Both of these elements were quickly assimilated by the Institute, and have become standard and valued practice.

Master of Studies Programmes

To enhance the practical relevance of criminology while promoting high-quality research was one of the main goals during the directorship of Anthony Bottoms. Among its most visible results are the two Master of Studies programmes in applied criminology.

In the 1990s the University of Cambridge, belatedly catching up with other universities, for the first time offered the possibility of awarding a postgraduate degree based on part-time study. In most universities, this would have been done by simply making the existing Master's degree (in our case, the MPhil) available to part-time students, since the required academic standard was the same. But Cambridge University does not always choose the expected path, and so it was decided that the new degree would be known as a 'Master of Studies' (or MSt) degree. The MSt has no explicit residential requirement, though specified hours of supervised teaching and learning are essential. Many Cambridge departments have shown little enthusiasm for embracing such courses. In contrast, Anthony Bottoms recognised the unique chance for Criminology to develop a vibrant part-time programme for criminal justice managers.

From its earliest days the Institute had been engaged in the teaching of those working in the criminal justice system through the 'Senior Course', which had become a biennial event. However, this teaching, although by common consent very valuable, was based on a single short course, and it did not lead to any recognised qualification. The opportunity to create a Master's programme arose in the mid-1990s when the then Director of National Police Training, Peter Ryan, approached the Institute to ask whether it could assist with the training of police officers on the national Strategic Command Course, the gateway to promotion to the rank of Assistant Chief Constable. The story of this programme is told more fully in chapter 3, along with that of the parallel MSt programme in penological studies, aimed especially at managers in the prison and probation services, which began a couple of years later. Both programmes have now been running for over a decade, and they have become a well-established and successful element in the Institute's overall teaching profile. For a time, the Senior Course continued to run alongside the MSt courses, but it has now been discontinued, leaving the MSt courses as the flagship courses for the Institute's longstanding mission to build bridges with the world of criminal justice practice.

A World-Leading Research Institute in a New Millennium: 1999–2009

At the end of 1998, Anthony Bottoms resigned as Director in order to concentrate on his research. He was succeeded by Michael Tonry, a prominent American specialist in criminal law and public policy, who directed the Institute for the following five years (1999–2004). It was the significant achievement of Michael Tonry during this period to finalise the financial package for the Institute's long-promised new building, and then to work with the architects (Allies and Morrison) in overseeing every aspect of its design and completion, from initial sketches to the transfer of the Institute's work from No. 7 West Road in 2004. From 2005, Michael Tonry was succeeded by Friedrich Lösel, the current Director of the Institute, from the University of Erlangen-Nuremberg in Bavaria, who has a wide range of research interests in criminology, clinical psychology, psychology and law, assessment, and programme evaluation. His immediate tasks were filling the Institute's new home with the appropriate spirit and consolidating the budget of the programmes in applied criminology.

A further senior appointment made in these years was the election of Lawrence Sherman as the fourth Wolfson Professor of Criminology after the retirement of Anthony Bottoms in 2006. Like his predecessor, Sherman is an alumnus of the Institute, having studied on the Diploma course in 1972–3. He subsequently returned to his native USA, where he became known, in particular, as a leading scholar in the field of police research, and as an active pioneer and proponent of experimental criminology.

Developing a European Criminology

For many decades in the second half of the 20th century, almost no avenues existed to promote the exchange of research and knowledge amongst criminologists across Europe. Maybe ironically, it was the American Michael Tonry who both strengthened the European links of the Institute and contributed to the development of a genuinely European criminology. As a Visiting Professor of the University of Lausanne (since 2001) and a Senior Fellow of the Netherlands Institute for the Study of Crime and Law Enforcement (NSCR, since 2003) he encouraged cooperation amongst some of the leading criminology departments in Europe. Also, together with a sizeable delegation of Cambridge academics (David Farrington, Per-Olof Wikström, and

Staff and students in the old Institute library at 7 West Road, 1969. Leon Radzinowicz (Sir Leon was knighted in 1970) is seated in the centre with his colleague, Professor Marvin Wolfgang (University of Pennsylvania), to his left. He and Wolfgang collaborated on the advice to the Home Office on violence after the abolition of capital punishment. To his right sits Mrs Wolfgang and, next to her, Donald West. Derick McClintock is seated at the extreme right of the front row next to the then Mrs Radzinowicz. Martin Wright, the librarian, is standing directly behind Radzinowicz and on the back row are David Farrington (second from left), Gerry Rose (third from left), Anthony Bottoms (fourth from left), Keith Hawkins (fifth from left) and Dick Sparks (sixth from left).

Manuel Eisner), he was actively involved in initiating the European Society of Criminology in 2000, and this body has since become by far the most important professional association for criminologists in Europe.

This strategy of actively promoting cooperation amongst European criminologists has been continued by Friedrich Lösel, who, with his strong Continental connections is, of course, well placed to do so. Amongst other things, recent years have seen the establishment of a network of leading European criminology institutes, comprising, as well as our own Institute, the NSCR in the Netherlands, the Max-Planck Institute for International and Comparative Criminal Law in Freiburg im Breisgau and the Institute of Criminology in Heidelberg.

A Global Perspective

In various ways, the Institute also increasingly defines itself as a research institution that combines a national mission with a global perspective in research and teaching. This is reflected in an increasingly international academic staff and a vibrant community of doctoral students and postdoctoral Fellows from various parts of the world.

Also, this shift can be seen in all of the Institute's postgraduate programmes, whose participants are recruited from amongst the most motivated and talented students across the world. For example, in the years 2000–9 the MPhil programme has received applications from some 70 countries (see Table p.28). In particular, the Institute is proud to regularly attract students from Africa, South America and South East Asia, thus contributing to the furthering of criminology in developing countries.

Furthermore, over the past ten years the Institute has been fortunate to host some of the world's leading criminologists from a variety of countries as Visiting Fellows and scholars (see chapter 10).

Building Research Centres

With a view to professionalising research, institutionalising research specialisms, and promoting excellence Michael Tonry encouraged the foundation of research centres within the Institute,

Country of Origin of MPhil Applicants, 2000–9

UK	206	Italy	6	Denmark	2
USA	80	Iran	6	Colombia	2
Canada	27	Germany	6	Belgium	2
Pakistan	23	Jamaica	5	Bangladesh	2
Japan	20	Uganda	4	Austria	2
Australia	20	Sweden	4	Yugoslavia (FRY)	1
India	17	Spain	4	Tanzania	1
Ghana	17	Saudi Arabia	4	Puerto Rico	1
China	17	Portugal	4	Peru	1
Ireland	16	Macedonia (FYROM)	4	Maldives	1
Zambia	15	Ukraine	3	Luxembourg	1
Greece	15	Sri Lanka	3	Lithuania	1
Nigeria	11	Romania	3	Liberia	1
Croatia	10	Poland	3	Israel	1
South Korea	9	Hungary	3	Finland	1
Hong Kong	9	Brazil	3	Fiji	1
South Africa	8	Trinidad	2	Chile	1
Singapore	8	Thailand	2	Cameroon	1
Netherlands	8	Switzerland	2	Cambodia	1
Cyprus	8	Serbia	2	Bosnia-Herzegovina	1
Turkey	7	New Zealand	2	Republic of Belarus	1
Malaysia	7	Mexico	2	Argentina	1
France	7	Kosovo	2		
Norway	6	Kenya	2		

a policy that has been continued by the current Director. As a result the Institute currently has four research centres, namely the Prisons Research Centre (directed by Alison Liebling), the Centre for Penal Theory and Penal Ethics (directed by Andrew von Hirsch), the Peterborough Adolescent and Young Adult Development Study (PADS+, directed by Per-Olof Wikström), and the Jerry Lee Centre for Experimental Criminology (directed by Lawrence Sherman). These are more fully discussed in chapter 6.

Expanding Research Activities

The Institute has come a long way since the days when the Home Office was seen as the sole source of research funding. Sources of funding now include both national and international foundations and agencies. Currently the Institute is able to secure between £1.2–1.5 million of research funds each year, allowing it to contribute to significant basic and applied research across many subfields of criminology.

Extending Staff Numbers

Leon Radzinowicz (1988, pp.126–8) concluded his account of the early days of the Institute with some expressions of anxiety about the overall size of the Institute. He stated that at the outset the University thought the Institute should be small: a Director, four or five tenure-track University staff, and the Librarian. He noted, however, that 26 years later the permanent academic establishment of the Institute (excluding the Librarian) was still only six, so 'it is virtually the same size as when it was set up'. This he considered insufficient for an Institute claiming to fulfil the role and responsibilities of a world-class centre of excellence in criminology.

Successive Directors have shared Radzinowicz's concerns on this issue, and most would agree with him that, by now, a doubling of the original size of the Institute's establishment would have been desirable. But it has not been achieved. During the Directorship of Anthony Bottoms, two new University posts were created (currently held by Manuel Eisner and Loraine Gelsthorpe), so the present permanent establishment is eight. Some further enhancement has been achieved because the setting-up of the MSt courses has required the appointment of new staff, but these posts are not on the University's permanent establishment. During the Directorship of Friedrich Lösel, the Institute was able to establish an urgently-needed academic-related post for IT services, although the current financial climate does not offer much hope for further quick expansion. Therefore, among the justifiable celebrations of the Institute's achievements at this time of Jubilee, it is right to point to residual problems.

Conclusion

At the conclusion of his speech on the day of the formal opening of the Institute's new building in May 2005, Anthony Bottoms, once more acting as Director for a few months after Michael Tonry's departure, commented on what he described as the 'contrast between this wonderful building and some of the conditions and situations that, as professional criminologists, we routinely encounter when we are doing our research'. He continued:

> As criminologists, we visit run-down social housing areas where the residents are genuinely worried about crime levels and antisocial behaviour. We meet offenders who have grown up with every kind of structural and personal disadvantage, and we meet victims who have been psychologically scarred for life. We visit prisons where conditions are still not as the prison authorities would want them to be, and we observe court proceedings that even victims sometimes experience as alien. As academic analysts, inevitably we have to study such things with at least a degree of detachment, but as human beings we are quite properly significantly moved by many of these situations. It is vital that we retain that sense of involvement, even as we retain our high academic standards. A beautiful building like this is a place to reflect on, to understand better, and perhaps to try to change such things. It is not a place to ignore them.

It is very encouraging to be able to report that very substantial progress has been made in criminological explanation and understanding in the last half century. The Institute of Criminology has, of course, been by no means the only contributor to this progress, but it can reasonably claim to have played a vital part. The Institute also remains optimistic about the possibilities for future progress in the better understanding of crime and criminal justice. It is very conscious, however, of two things: first, that much still remains to be done, and secondly, that in carrying out its mission it owes a significant responsibility to those – frequently the disadvantaged – who suffer from the misery that crime can often bring in its wake.

The account in this chapter has however touched only lightly on a further vital dimension of the Institute's first half-century, namely the very generous benefactions and support that it has received. These are discussed fully in chapter 12, as a fitting conclusion to this volume.

Chapter 2

People Matter – The Institute's Staff

O ne of the key results of research on the day-to-day functioning of prisons is that 'staff matter' – indeed, the way that the staff treat prisoners is usually more important in prisoners' perceptions of their wellbeing than are the physical facilities or the details of the daily regime. Without wishing to draw over-close comparisons between the Institute and a prison, it is striking that in the reminiscences of alumni it is often one or more staff members who stand out as having 'made a difference' in students' experience – and the staff members who come into this category are by no means restricted to academics.

At the end of this chapter, we include brief biographical vignettes of seven leading figures in the first 50 years of the Institute's life – all the Wolfson Professors and the Directors. But of course, over the years there have been many other staff who have had distinctive and important roles to play.

Turning first to academic staff, for most of its history the Institute – along with other Cambridge University departments – has had to work with a sharp distinction between 'University Officers' (UOs), who hold tenured or tenure-track appointments, and other academic staff who are on fixed-term contracts. (This distinction still exists, but it has in practice become of considerably reduced significance following recent changes in employment law). Limited-term academic staff have belonged to two main categories – research staff working on Institute research projects, and in more recent years teaching staff for the Diploma/Master of Studies courses.

Tenured UO posts have usually been greatly prized, and staff turnover among this group has been low. Indeed, in the first half-century only 25 people have held such posts (see table on page 32). The four earliest UOs were Leon Radzinowicz, Donald West (see biographies), Derick McClintock and John Martin (see chapter 1). They were quickly followed by Joan King, a historian and former probation officer who assisted Leon Radzinowicz with the fourth volume of his *History*, and other publications, and who was the mainstay of the Institute's teaching on probation-related topics for many years. Other UO appointees a little later in the Radzinowicz era were Robert (Bob) Morrison, a former prison psychologist who was Deputy Director of the Institute for a short time before moving on to become the first Director of NACRO; two Institute PhD alumni, Roger Hood and the American Richard (Dick) Sparks (see chapters 1 and 9), who collaborated on an influential early review of research called *Key Issues in Criminology* (Hood and Sparks 1970); David Thomas, who was recruited from LSE soon after the publication of his path-breaking book *Principles of Sentencing* (1970); and the statistician/methodologist Gerry Rose, who left the Institute to go to Australia for many years before returning to a post at LSE – but after his return he has also assisted the Institute with research and teaching on many occasions. Some also remember fondly that, in Gerry's days at the Institute, at a time when authors always used only initials, he solved the problem of differentiating himself from the well-established Gordon Rose of Manchester by signing a couple of his articles 'G.N.G. Rose' – that is, 'Gerry Not Gordon Rose'! Significant non-tenured staff of this early period included the

Garret Hostel Bridge during May Week.

Academic Staff who have held University Officer posts

Trevor Bennett	Friedrich Lösel	Colin Sumner
Anthony Bottoms	F.H. McClintock	David Thomas
Manuel Eisner	John Martin	Michael Tonry
David Farrington	Allison Morris	Andrew von Hirsch
Loraine Gelsthorpe	Robert Morrison	Nigel Walker
Adrian Grounds	Leon Radzinowicz	Donald West
Roger Hood	Gerry Rose	Per-Olof Wikström
Joan King	Lawrence Sherman	
Alison Liebling	Richard F. Sparks	

psychologist Tony Gibson, who worked on the Cambridge Study in Delinquent Development, co-authoring many publications with Donald West; and Hazel Genn who worked with Dick Sparks on his pioneering UK victim study (see chapter 1) before moving on to a distinguished career in socio-legal studies which has seen her become Professor of Socio-Legal Studies at University College London, a Fellow of the British Academy, and a Dame Commander of the Order of the British Empire.

The years of the Directorships of Nigel Walker and Donald West (see biographies) saw three tenured appointments. David Farrington (see chapter 5), like Gerry Rose before him and several afterwards, moved from the Institute's unestablished staff to a UO position, and he subsequently became one of the Institute's most distinguished staff members. Juvenile justice specialist Allison Morris, recruited from Edinburgh, subsequently introduced the Institute's first course on feminist perspectives in criminology, and sociologist Colin Sumner 'radicalised' the MPhil course with Marxist-inspired thinking. One of Nigel Walker's unestablished appointees, Trevor Bennett, also became a longstanding staff member. For a decade, he conducted a series of externally-financed research studies (including a rigorous evaluation of neighbourhood watch schemes that the then government deliberately published on local election day, in order to divert public attention from its negative findings). Then in 1990 he was appointed to a new UO post in policing and crime prevention. He later became the first Director of the Police Diploma/MSt course, made major contributions to quantitative methods teaching, and was both Deputy and Acting Director for a short while before moving to the University of Glamorgan to take up a chair.

During the Directorship of Anthony Bottoms (see biography), Adrian Grounds arrived to replace Donald West and to develop the links between Forensic Psychiatry and Criminology (see chapter 4). In 1994, Loraine Gelsthorpe transferred from the unestablished research staff to a second new tenured post, this one focused especially on qualitative methods. Soon afterwards, the appointment of Per-Olof Wikström from Stockholm (to replace Colin Sumner) began what some have described as a recent 'European turn' in appointments to the Institute. To these UO appointments the Institute was fortunate also to add an election to an Honorary Professorship in Penal Theory and Penal Law, created for the distinguished penal philosopher Andrew von Hirsch, who came to Cambridge from Rutgers University, New Jersey, but who also has strong links with German and Swedish universities. Among unestablished staff in this period were Richard Sparks, later a successor to Derick McClintock in the Edinburgh Chair of Criminology; John Pratt, now a professor in New Zealand and a specialist in the sociology of

Three of the four Wolfson Professors. Anthony Bottoms, then the incumbent Professor, with his predecessors, Nigel Walker and Sir Leon Radzinowicz. The photograph was taken by David Thomas on the occasion of a dinner to celebrate Sir Leon's 90th birthday in 1996.

penal systems; and William (Bill) McWilliams, after whose death in 1997 his friends established in his honour an annual lecture on a probation-related topic, some of which have been hosted at the Institute.

More recent UO appointments have, of course, seen the appointments of Michael Tonry and Friedrich Lösel as Directors, and Lawrence Sherman as the fourth Wolfson Professor (see biographies). Additionally, Alison Liebling, already on the Institute's research staff, replaced David Thomas (see chapter 6); and Manuel Eisner from Switzerland replaced Trevor Bennett as a quantitative methods specialist, though he also brings with him a welcome renaissance of the Institute's tradition of historical research (see chapter 7).

The 1990s also saw the creation of the Applied Diploma and MSt courses, and this required the appointment of several new staff. On the police MSt, the Institute initially benefited from the scholarship, teaching and enthusiasm of Ben Bowling and Janet Foster, who both in due course

left to take up permanent positions in London (Ben to King's College, where he now holds a chair, and Janet to the LSE). On the prisons/penology side, the initial Director of the course (working alongside Alison Liebling) was Nicola Padfield, who remained in this position until she gained a University Lectureship in her parent discipline, and moved across the Sidgwick Site to the Law Faculty. Later unestablished appointments connected more or less closely with the MSt have included Shadd Maruna, an American academic whose work on narratives of redemption has become internationally known, and who is now at Queen's University Belfast; also Amanda Matravers from Keele and Professor Roy King, a 'retiree' from Bangor and an internationally-acknowledged authority in prison studies, who came to direct the Police and Penology courses respectively. Tim Coupe became the Institute's first in-house teacher in management studies, which to his great credit he has been able to combine with criminological research. Mandeep Dhami and Katrin Müller-Johnson have significantly strengthened the Institute's research profile in legal psychology, specialising in decision-making and in eyewitness testimony respectively. Others who have maintained the more traditional primary research focus of unestablished research staff include two Senior Research Associates – Kate Painter, who has specialised in work on crime prevention and more recently terrorism, and Ben Crewe whose work in the Prisons Research Centre has included nuanced ethnographic studies of prison life under contemporary conditions of stricter security and control. The Institute has also benefitted from the move to Cambridge of Elizabeth Burney, a well-known criminological researcher from London who has become a part-time Senior Research Fellow and has contributed greatly to the Institute's work, especially in the fields of housing and crime, incivilities and Anti-Social Behaviour Orders, and racial harassment. Other staff make significant contributions as research project staff or postdoctoral Fellows.

Librarian Helen Krarup (left) and Pam Paige (centre), PA to Tony Bottoms throughout his time as Director, on the Backs.

34

Library staff

The Radzinowicz Library is in many ways the most public face of the Institute, and it is a place that is fondly remembered by many former staff, students and visitors (see chapter 8). Successive Librarians have tended to care most about creating an atmosphere of friendly and efficient service to all users, rather than emphasising the Library's undeniable merits as a research collection – and this ethos has become a very precious asset to the Institute.

The Institute owes a huge debt to successive Librarians and library staff. Among Librarians, outstanding professional service was given successively in the early years by Joan Friedman and then Martin Wright (see chapters 1 and 8), and subsequently by Rosina Perry before her departure for Australia. The Library's most colourful character in the early years was undoubtedly Isobel Gawler, a friendly but formidable lady who was among other things a superb proof-reader. In those days the library's materials on sex crimes and the like were kept in the 'confidential cupboard', to which Miss Gawler held the keys – and this deterred not a few would-be applicants!

In later years, as Librarian, Stephen Gregory carefully tended the Institute's library traditions, but he was more at home in the worlds of history and theology, to which he eventually returned. During this period Jean Taylor and Betty Arnold were, technically, respectively Senior Library Assistant and Library Secretary, but in fact they worked as an excellent and longstanding double-act. They could provide useful responses to the vaguest of requests from academics and students, and sometimes even name a book by its colour and size! Working alongside them as a part-time evening invigilator and bookbinder was Michael Frattasi, originally recruited in the Radzinowicz era, who at one point was the longest-serving member of staff of the Institute.

After some rapid changes in the post of Librarian, Helen Krarup took up that office in 1992 from a background as a member of the Institute's research staff. At a vital moment in the Library's history, she provided stability, criminological knowledge and a determination to move the Library into the digital age, and the Institute owes her a great deal. She also in due course recruited Mary Gower and Stuart Stone to replace Jean Taylor and Betty Arnold, and happily both are still with us, maintaining the Library's traditions. In 2005, when Helen Krarup retired, Mary became the first member of the Institute's library staff to be promoted to the post of Librarian. Earlier, Helen Krarup had planned, with the architects, the detailed configuration of the Library in the new building, and Mary Gower was principally responsible for the complicated logistics of the move.

Behind the scenes

Behind every successful academic in the Institute, there is a team of very able and loyal administrative and support staff. The Institute has been exceptionally lucky in attracting staff who have not only understood but who have shared its aims and aspirations – whether this be to do with maintaining routine administrative matters to enable academic staff to get on with research and teaching, participating in the careful stewardship of resources, creating ways of increasing the profile of the Institute both within and beyond the University, guiding students to the right place, entertaining the children of visitors, or providing a shoulder to cry on (for both students and staff on occasion). They are too numerous to acknowledge them all, and so focusing on the 1980s onwards in particular, this chapter would not be complete without mention of Margaret Guy as Administrative Officer who provided clear administrative leadership for a good number of years, Pat Cochrane who managed the MPhil course for many years, Joan Clegg who managed the accounts – and anxious PhD students on the side, and Pam Paige, officially the Director's Secretary but sometimes known as the 'Institute Mum' for her natural charm and encouragement which often made the impossible seem possible. Later, there was incoming support from Thelma Norman (transferring from another academic department) and Tisha Hug (coming in from the world of business), successive Administrative Officers for the Institute following Margaret Guy's return to education to take a degree. (Tisha also provided an Institute mascot in the form of 'Lottie', a small terrier – the sort of thing that is possible in an old house but not in a gleaming new building!). Jean Kenworthy became the accounts officer, and Maureen Brown the receptionist. Christmas carols in the library and the notable efforts of senior professors to sing a verse at the Christmas Dinner under the command of Maureen are memorable. Maureen continues to 'babysit' in Reception on occasions when Joanne Garner is away. Sara Harrop made major impact in her work as PA to then Director, Michael Tonry, and until recently continued to work on the European Society of Criminology Newsletter in her spare time, even though she has now moved on to a different department in the University.

Tisha Hug with 'Lottie'.

In 1999, on the resignation of Tisha Hug for personal reasons, the Institute was at last deemed important enough by the University to warrant the upgrading of its principal administrative post. Three people have so far held this new office – Linda Whitebread, who held the post for 18 months before moving to work at the Board of Graduate Studies; Ken McCormick, whose particular interest and skills lay in ensuring a smooth move to the new building, and in ironing out teething problems with the building when we arrived; and Caroline Edwards, who has brought Northern good sense, new skills and an attitude of support to everybody in the Institute who needs her help.

Among present staff, Joanne Garner's official title is that of Institute Receptionist, but she also provides excellent secretarial support to a number of staff and manages the publicity for the seminars and some conferences. In many ways she is the public face of the Institute – attentive to all enquirers and no problem is too great for her to deal with. Excellent technical services are provided by Computer Officer Matt Skipper (treading in the footsteps of the equally excellent Roger Price). Richard Davey as Senior Accounts Officer and Lisa Porteous as Accounts Clerk provide an efficient service. Lisa also doubles up in the Personnel Office as part of a job-share with Michelle Talbot. The graduate teaching programmes have skilful and energetic support in the form of administrators Lucinda Bowditch (for the Applied Criminology programmes) and Catherine Byfield (for the MPhil and PhD Programmes). Centre administrators too have played a key role in the Institute's development, Ann Phillips in particular, who provides administrative support in the Prisons Research Centre (along with Jennifer Cartwright) and also the Penal Theory Centre, while Anne-Helene Halbout is administrator on the PADS+ project. Finally, we are now in the fortunate position of having staff to look after the building with former Metropolitan Police officer John Adams MBE as Chief Custodian and Arnel Badayos as Custodian. Naomi Young is the most recent addition to the Institute's key staff, as the Director's Personal Assistant.

Biographies of Directors and Wolfson Professors

Sir Leon Radzinowicz

Arriving alone in London in 1936 to write a report for the Polish government, Leon Radzinowicz carefully linked into the social networks of people making crime and justice policy – starting with the top civil servant at the Home Office, who endorsed his review of British crime policy. He also connected with the Howard League for Penal Reform, one of whose Board Members was J.W.C. Turner, a Fellow of Trinity Hall, Cambridge. With his European education and publications, his precocious honours from the King of Belgium, and a warm reference from Howard League Secretary, Cicely Craven, the 30-year-old Leon was met by Cecil Turner at Cambridge station on a sunny afternoon. On that day, British criminology hit what Malcolm Gladwell has termed 'the tipping point'.

Over lunch, a walk and dinner, Turner and Radzinowicz spoke broadly about a wide range of issues in criminal law. By dinnertime, the usually reticent Turner invited Radzinowicz to come to Cambridge 'to help me expand the study of crime and punishment'. By 1940, the Cambridge Law Faculty had established a standing committee to consider the promotion of 'criminal science,' with our founder becoming the unpaid (and unofficial) secretary of the committee. At a time when, as he wrote, 'criminologists were looked upon with greater suspicion than criminals,' young Leon was 'on probation.' He spent the next decade earning his way off probation and into a Fellowship at Trinity College by dint of three achievements: (i) a series of publications with J.W.C. Turner showing the relevance of criminology for criminal law; (ii) a series of meetings at Cambridge he organised with justice and interior officials of European governments in exile; and (iii) an early article on the reform of English crime policy since 1760, which won him the strong support of Law Faculty Chairman and Trinity Fellow H.A. Hollond, followed by the award-winning first volume of his *magnum opus* on the same history that won him the support of the Master of Trinity, the historian G.M. Trevelyan.

Herein lie three solutions to the mystery as to why a scientific criminologist whose previous publications had analysed a wide range of statistics on crime and social conditions made his name in Britain as a legal historian. One solution is that he discovered in Cambridge libraries a treasure trove of archives on two centuries of penal reform: Parliamentary debates and 'blue book' Royal Commissions, in particular. As Thurgood Marshall wanted to have it said of himself, Radzinowicz 'did the best he could with what he had.' Lacking resources or official blessings for field research, he turned documents into data that had never been analysed.

The second solution is found in Edwin Sutherland's definition of criminology as the study of law-making, law-breaking and reactions to law-breaking. Given the massive imbalance of our field tilting towards the last two of these three parts, Radzinowicz pioneered the study of law-making on the most central issue: reactions to law-breaking. Few knew, before his work, that all prosecutions had once been privately funded, that proposals to create a police force had been repeatedly rejected for over half a century, and that the death penalty had been widely applied to minor crimes until shortly before the police were created. Like the early explorers of the oceans and continents, Sir Leon gave us a map of the unknown world called the (recent) past.

The third and most important solution reflects Sir Leon's social intelligence. The study of history had powerful allies at Cambridge; criminology did not. By demonstrating the importance of criminology as a lens for viewing history, Radzinowicz made the study of crime intellectually respectable. That, in turn, pulled him more deeply into the social networks of academic policy, where he personified the means to create the new Department of Criminal Science in 1941 and the Institute of Criminology two decades later. As Gladwell suggests, a sudden and major change often reflects the work of a few extraordinary people. Like Churchill, Sir Leon's extraordinary knack was to use the writing of history to help make it.

(For a fuller and more formal biography of Sir Leon, see Hood, R. [2001] 'Leon Radzinowicz 1906–99'. *Proceedings of the British Academy III*, 637–55, also Sir Leon's autobiographical *Adventures in Criminology* [1999]).

Nigel Walker

Nigel Walker attributes much of his success in life to luck: see his so-called 'afterthoughts', *A Man without Loyalties* (Walker 2003). It is perhaps typical that it is left to those who worked with him, or studied under him, to appreciate his talents: an incisive mind, an eye for detail, and a no-nonsense approach which made him an invaluable committee member and an inspirational teacher. The 'afterthoughts' provide a fascinating insight into his life, with details of his early childhood in northern China, his school days in Edinburgh and undergraduate studies at Oxford (where he won the Chancellor's Prize for his Latin poem in 1936). He describes his 15 years as a lucky but bored bureaucrat in the Scottish Office, which he left for the University of Oxford in 1961. He became Wolfson Professor of Criminology, Director of the Institute, and a Fellow of King's College in 1973. He stepped down as Director of the Institute in 1981, and retired from his Professorship in 1984, but stayed in Cambridge for many more years before retiring to Edinburgh.

Nigel is admired in particular for the astonishing clarity of his writing, his wise and highly influential contributions to policy debates and for his careful encouragement of students and colleagues. He made his name in academic criminology (although there were previous books on other subjects) with *Crime and Punishment in Britain* (1965), and the two-volume *Crime and Insanity in England* (1968). His books written primarily for students are masterly communications, incisive, meticulous and wide-ranging. He demonstrated, always with great precision, flaws in popular penal theories, specialising in awkward questions: his *Punishment, Danger and Stigma: The Morality of Criminal Justice* (1980), for example, is a typical hard-hitting call for moral arguments based on practicalities rather than (blind) faith.

Throughout his time in Cambridge he was very busy on national committees. It was a heady time of reform. He chaired the Home Secretary's Advisory Council on probation and aftercare 1972–6, and was a member of the Advisory Council on the Penal System 1969–73, the (Butler) Committee on mentally abnormal offenders 1972–5, the working party on judicial training and information 1975–8, the Howard League's (Floud) Committee on dangerous offenders and its (Hodgson) Committee on profits of crime. After his retirement, he served on the Parole Board 1986–9. His capacity to blend theory and practice was perhaps unique. As Michael Davis (1993, p. 395–405) wrote, 'Walker is a social scientist who takes theory seriously enough to try to test it against practice. …he is a student of practice no theorist can safely ignore'. Despite his place on the national penal stage, for which he was awarded the CBE, he found plenty of time for students, and for making the Institute an efficient, happy and effective place. He cherished debate. The group discussions he organised for students and prisoners in Bedford Prison, as well as his seminar classes, were seminal events for many of those working in the field today. He encouraged students of theory not to ignore the reality and practice of punishment.

Nigel Walker, Emeritus Wolfson Professor of Criminology, 1973– 1984, and Director of the Institute 1973–81.

There is no pretension about Nigel, and he valued every person's contribution. His quiet empathy brought out the best in those who struggled to understand penal philosophy and the barriers to penal reform, though the sharpness of his mind permitted him to knock down pretension in others.

His influence will be felt for many years, and not just in the annual Nigel Walker Lecture, established in his honour (see chapter 1). A small example: his article 'The End of an Old Song' (Walker 1999) was, only recently, the focus of some debate in the courts. Nigel took the view that it was at least arguable that section 34 of the Crime and Disorder Act 1998 had not abolished the rebuttable presumption of *doli incapax* (that a child aged between ten and 14 years could not form the necessary criminal intent for criminal liability). He noted that during the second reading of the Bill, the Solicitor General had said that the change would only remove the presumption and would not rule out the possibility that a child with 'genuine learning difficulties and who is genuinely at sea on the question of right and wrong' would be able to run *doli incapax* as a defence. The first judicial consideration of the matter was not until *CPS v P* [2007] EWHC 946 (admin) where Smith L.J. concluded that 'there was much to be said for the view expressed by Professor Walker', but sadly her tentative conclusions were not adopted by the Court of Appeal in *R v T* [2008] EWCA Crim 815. Nonetheless, it was pleasing to see Nigel provoke a lively debate once again (and once again, he should have won the argument!).

Donald West

Donald West's introduction to the Institute of Criminology, on 1 January 1960, was to say the least unusual. Following a successful informal interview with Leon Radzinowicz at the Athenaeum, he moved to Cambridge and made a disconcerting discovery:

> *Certainly he gave me to understand that I was appointed ... But I was not appointed. I arrived at the Institute ... when it was in Scroope Terrace, on 1st January…, the date that he had required me to be there and, of course, everything was closed up and snow was on the ground. And it emerged that he had not been through the appropriate appointment arrangements and the Appointments Committee hadn't met, and didn't in fact ratify his recommendation for six months or more, until I was finally paid. And I remember him saying – I went to see him in his house ... pointing to some expensive carpeting, he'd sell the carpet if I didn't get paid ... He was always doing things like that … jumping the gun, you know.*
>
> (Extract from interview with Donald West, December 2008)

This inauspicious start did not prevent Donald West from being a tower of strength in the Institute for the next quarter-century. His huge contributions are set out in the chapters on forensic psychiatry and the Cambridge Study in Delinquent Development (see chs 4 and 5), and need not be repeated here. He was justifiably promoted to a personal Professorship in Clinical Criminology in 1979, at a time when Cambridge was extremely sparing in its conferral of such awards. He also served as Director of the Institute for the three years 1981–4, between the Directorships of Nigel Walker and Tony Bottoms. Donald West frankly admitted in later years that he did not particularly enjoy the role of Director, and he regarded himself 'as a kind of caretaker' (interview with Donald West, December 2008). Unfortunately, the short period was not without stress: he recalled a particularly difficult occasion when a student failed the course, complained and an enquiry was established, during which evidence was discovered of an office break-in and the insertion into the student's file of an apparently forged letter. The student was eventually prosecuted and imprisoned.

Interestingly, the work that Donald West himself considers to be of the most importance, both personally and for social policy, was his Penguin book on *Homosexuality*, published in 1955 before he came to the Institute. This already had the features of his later work: the careful analysis of evidence – anthropological, statistical, and psychological – combined with a concern for reform. The evidence made a compelling case for the normality, decriminalisation and social acceptance of homosexuality. It was a brave and influential book, written at a time when consensual homosexual relationships were legally proscribed and therefore hidden. In America the title was altered by the publisher to *The Other Man*, and in Australia copies were confiscated by customs officials as obscene. The book contributed significantly to a gradual change in attitudes and policy, and to the recommendations of the Wolfenden Report (Home Office 1957) that, as Donald West later put it 'helped to direct critical attention to the shaky assumptions that lay behind anti-homosexual legislation' (West 1977, p.285). But it took a further decade before legislative reform was eventually achieved through the passing of the Sexual Offences Act 1967.

When talking recently about the book, Donald West reflected on its importance for his generation:

> ... in my old age I'm surprised to have met numbers of people – gay people I mean – who have told me that it helped them in their early days to read something which suggested they were more or less normal instead of being outside the pale ... and they found that very comforting. ... I think it contributed, and so I'm proud of that.

(INTERVIEW, DECEMBER 2008)

Sir Anthony Bottoms

Anthony Bottoms learned his criminology at the Institute as a member of the first postgraduate course, and subsequently as a research officer working with Derick McClintock (1964–8). He was therefore no stranger to Cambridge when he was elected as the third Wolfson Professor of Criminology in 1984, having spent the previous 16 years helping to establish criminology at the University of Sheffield. He held the Wolfson Professorship until 2006, and also served as Director of the Institute of Criminology from 1984 to 1998.

Tony Bottoms's research interests are wide-ranging, and include desistance from crime (see Bottoms 2006), socio-spatial criminology (see Bottoms and Costello 2009), penology and theoretical criminology. He has particular interests in social order, morality and legal compliance. His unusually wide range of interests enabled him to play a hugely significant role in research leadership at the Institute as well as to publish (for example) *Prisons and the Problem of Order* (with Richard Sparks and Will Hay 1996), and a series of long, elegant essays on, amongst other things, crime and insecurity in the city, the aims of imprisonment, the relationship between theory and research in criminology, sentencing theory, morality, crime and compliance,

Donald West, Emeritus Professor of Clinical Criminology and instigator of the Cambridge Study in Delinquent Development, Director of the Institute of Criminology, 1981–4, at home in London in December 2008, with 19th-century souvenirs of famous criminological events. (From left to right: Stansfield Hall, the scene of a famous Victorian murder; The Titchbourne Claimant, an imposter who sought fraudulently to inherit a fortune; and Sir James Rush, a murderer who defended himself unsuccessfully and was hanged).

alternatives to custody, restorative justice, deterrence and community penalties. During his time as Director he worked in close partnership with younger colleagues in developing their research careers, and also with the Law Faculty, building mutually rewarding relationships and expanding the permanent staff of the Institute from six to eight. He negotiated with the University over a long period to ensure that the overdue commitment to provide the Institute with a suitable permanent home would be honoured (see further chapter 11). Professor Bottoms continued to supervise undergraduate, postgraduate and PhD students throughout his period as Director, often personally encouraging and mentoring outstanding students from disadvantaged backgrounds and under-represented countries. He also continued to conduct his own empirical research, and was thus able to provide methodological as well as conceptual advice to staff and students. The verb 'to Tonify' was coined in this period, referring to his exacting but always improving comments on the drafts of others' work. He found time also to be active in his college (Fitzwilliam), including a period as President (Deputy Master) from 1994 to 1998.

A meeting of the International Advisory Board of the Police Executive Programme chaired by Anthony Bottoms in the Sir Anthony Bottoms Room. July 2009.

Whilst he was Director, he pioneered the Institute's Diploma and Master of Studies (MSt) courses for senior police officers and senior managers in the prisons and probation services. These highly successful courses attract senior operational practitioners eager to apply empirical and theoretical knowledge to their professional work. Professor Bottoms worked tirelessly to set the teaching standard, leading the highly successful and experimental syllabus design and giving more than his fair share of seminars on both programmes. His ease with practitioner audiences is rooted in the combined effects of his own professional experience (as a probation officer in the early 1960s) and his obvious and warm respect for all criminal justice practitioner personnel. Students responded with enthusiasm to apparently unusual topics such as 'structuration theory', or accounts of 'the characteristics of late modern societies', once they were encouraged to reflect on how these ideas could help to make sense of their professional experience.

Professor Bottoms has acted as a member of, or advisor to, a number of official and quasi-official bodies, including the Home Office Research and Advisory Group on the Long-Term Prison System (1984–90) and, on three occasions, the House of Commons Northern Ireland Affairs Committee for its inquiries into the Northern Ireland Prison Service (1998–2007). A report by him to the Scottish Executive also led directly to the establishment of the Scottish Centre for Crime and Justice Research, embracing several universities, in 2006.

It was entirely fitting that Anthony Bottoms was knighted for 'services to the Criminal Justice System' in 2001. He was also elected a Fellow of the British Academy in 1997, and has received several other honours, including honorary doctorates from Sheffield University and Queen's University, Belfast. In 2007, he was the first recipient of the European Society of Criminology's new lifetime achievement award.

His enduring interests in values and relationships permeated his style and activities as Director. The Institute decided to name its elegant new boardroom the 'Sir Anthony Bottoms Room' in his honour in 2007.

Michael Tonry

Michael Tonry was the first non-British citizen to be appointed as Director of the Institute in 1999. Energetic and restless, Michael's career had taken several different turns before he settled into the world of criminal justice. After a first degree in African history, he then studied law at Yale, where he became interested in anthropology through his holiday work at a poverty law clinic. This led to a further year at Yale in the anthropology department before joining a large corporate law firm in Chicago. Two years later in 1971, his real career beckoned when he was offered the job of administrator of the University of Chicago's Center for Studies in Criminal Justice, working with Professor Norval Morris, who became a lifelong friend.

Law teaching positions followed successively at Birmingham, England and the University of Maryland. In the late 1970s, Michael founded his own criminological research center (at Castine, Maine) at which he initiated (at first jointly with Norval Morris) his very influential yearbook of criminological and criminal-justice research, *Crime and Justice*. This series has run to nearly 40 volumes, and constitutes the best corpus of analyses of contemporary criminological research in existence. Its quality has been assured by Michael's ability to attract leading criminologists as contributors, his skill and dedication in revising and editing each contribution, and his encyclopaedic knowledge of the field of criminology.

In the early 1990s, Michael Tonry accepted the Sonosky Professorship of Law and Public Policy at the University of Minnesota, a position which he has maintained ever since. In 1999,

Michael Tonry, Professor of Law and Public Policy and Director of the Institute of Criminology, 1999–2004.

he was appointed Director and Professor at the Cambridge Institute of Criminology, where he served for the next five years. He returned to the University of Minnesota in 2004.

Michael Tonry is a leading authority worldwide in a number of important areas of research, including criminal sentencing and the regulation of sentencing discretion (Tonry 1996); the effects of criminal policies on minorities (Tonry 1995); and the impact of contemporary political trends on penal legislation and policy (Tonry 2004, 2006).

Tonry brought to his role as Director of the Institute his great energy and his interest in interdisciplinary approaches. He initiated the concept of research centres within the Institute, beginning with the Prisons Research Centre (directed by Alison Liebling) and the Centre for Penal Theory and Penal Ethics (directed by Andrew von Hirsch); to these was subsequently added the Research Network on Social Contexts of Pathways in Crime (SCoPiC) (directed by Per-Olof Wikström). He also continued Tony Bottoms' engagement in the two Master of Studies programmes, on police and corrections, at a time when they were both funded by central contracts with the relevant criminal justice agencies.

However, the most visible reminder of Michael Tonry's tenure as Director is, of course, the Institute's new building. The old quarters on West Road, in an extended Victorian villa of the 1870s, had long become cramped and decrepit. Notable efforts had been made by previous Directors to obtain University support for a new structure but on Michael's arrival in 1999, the Institute was still in the old building.

He negotiated University approval for a larger structure; and he obtained an enhanced funding commitment from the University and outside sources, which enabled the building plans to go ahead. He then worked with the architects (Allies and Morrison) on configuring the plans. The result is a remarkable achievement: the building is striking and elegantly designed, roomy and comfortable, and a great pleasure to work in. It is tangible testimony to the determination, energy and skill which Michael brought to bear on the task of directing the Institute over his five-year tenure.

Friedrich Lösel

When Friedrich Lösel became the sixth Director of the Institute in 2005, he was well-prepared to navigate among the diverse disciplines and methodologies represented by its academics and students. He grew up in Middle Franconia, a culturally and religiously mixed part of Bavaria located as a buffer between two very homogeneous – and quite different – areas. Professor Lösel learned at an early age how to solve problems by integrating competing perspectives, which has long been the major intellectual challenge for criminology.

As a gifted student of psychology, he earned his PhD in 1974 and his *habilitation* (the second PhD required for German professors) in 1978. He worked at Erlangen and Bamberg Universities and at two Advanced Research Centres of the German Research Council. After professorships at Erlangen and Bielefeld Universities he became Director of the Institute of Psychology at the University of Erlangen-Nuremberg in 1987, where he was later elected Dean of the Faculty of Philosophy, History, and Social Sciences. At the same time, he led path-breaking longitudinal studies, experiments and systematic evaluations of a wide range of strategies for challenging crime. Twenty-five books and 300 articles and chapters later, he has made major contributions in both English and German to the study of the prevention of juvenile delinquency, risk and protective factors in the development of aggression, school bullying, football hooliganism, the treatment and management of psychopaths and sex offenders, and the organisation of prisons.

The quality and impact of his work has been widely recognised by his many honours. In 2006, he was selected as the first co-recipient (with John Braithwaite of the Australian National University) of the Stockholm Prize in Criminology, an award established by the Swedish Ministry of Justice. In the same year, he received the German Psychology Award for outstanding achievements in psychological research and its application. Recognised by the American Society of Criminology by the Sellin-Glueck Award for outstanding contributions to international criminology, he was elected President of both the Criminological Society of the German-speaking Countries and the European Association of Psychology and Law. He also holds an Honorary Doctorate in Science from Glasgow Caledonian University.

In the best Cambridge Criminology tradition, Lösel has readily accepted many invitations to advise and work with governments. These include Germany's Anti-Violence Commission and review committees for correctional treatment programmes in the UK, Canada and Germany. Recently he chaired the Correctional Services Programme Accreditation Panel in England and Wales. More importantly, his work has helped to change the way in which governments think about crime prevention policy. His pioneering work on systematic reviews of rigorous evaluations of criminal justice treatment programmes led to an invitation to join the International Campbell Collaboration, which commissions reviews of crime prevention evaluations conducted all over the world. An elected Fellow of the Academy of Experimental Criminology, Lösel has strengthened the scientific side of the Institute's mission to link knowledge with public policy. Under his leadership, the MSt programmes in applied criminology initiated by Sir Anthony Bottoms have flourished and expanded.

Professor Lösel, a Fellow of Wolfson College, also excels at several other traditions of Cambridge Criminology. He invariably leaves the crowd laughing with witty remarks at any ceremonial occasion. He maintains an intense schedule of invited lectures linking Cambridge to the global academic and policy communities. He has strengthened the relationship between the Institute and its parent Law Faculty. He is committed to the highest standards of research and scholarship. And in his philosophy of crime prevention and intervention over the life course of human development, he retains a fundamental but realistic optimism. As he put it in the title of a recent article, 'It is never too early and never too late'.

Professor Friedrich Lösel, Director of the Institute since 2005, talking to Queen Sylvia of Sweden at the Stockholm Criminology Symposium in 2007 with Professor Hans-Jürgen Kerner, a former Visiting Fellow at the Institute and past President of the International Society of Criminology.

Lawrence Sherman

Lawrence Sherman came to the Institute of Criminology as a graduate student in 1972–3, after two years as a research analyst in the New York Police. He completed his PhD at Yale in 1976 with his mentor Albert Reiss, then taught at SUNY-Albany and the University of Maryland.

Appointed Greenfield Professor of Human Relations at the University of Pennsylvania in 1999, he founded its Jerry Lee Center of Criminology and the Ivy League's first department of criminology. He returned to Cambridge in 2007 as Wolfson Professor of Criminology and Director of the Police Executive Programme.

By the 1980s, Sherman was recognised as one of the leading researchers on policing. His 1984 paper with Richard Berk on the Minneapolis Domestic Violence Experiment was a landmark publication, followed by his 1989 paper on the spatial concentration of crime in 'hot spots,' his 1993 'Defiance Theory,' and his 1995 experiments on hot spot patrols (with David Weisburd) and gun crime prevention (with Dennis Rogan). The Minneapolis Domestic Violence Experiment sparked the first systematic replication programme in the history of experimental criminology, with separate tests in six US cities. His 1992 book on these experiments, *Policing Domestic Violence*, was hailed as a masterpiece, winning the prestigious prize for distinguished scholarship from the American Sociological Association.

With his Maryland colleagues, Sherman directed the 1997 production of the landmark report on *Preventing Crime: What Works, What Doesn't, What's Promising*. Jerry Lee, a Philadelphia philanthropist, was so inspired by the report that he became the largest private donor in the history of criminology. After establishing the Jerry Lee Center of Criminology at the University of Pennsylvania in 2000, Sherman and Lee agreed in 2008 to establish the Jerry Lee Centre of Experimental Criminology at the Cambridge Institute of Criminology.

In the last decade, Sherman has made a major and long-lasting contribution to knowledge by encouraging the development of the Campbell Collaboration (www.campbellcollaboration. org), which publishes systematic reviews of the effectiveness of criminological interventions on the internet. He also founded the Academy of Experimental Criminology to foster experimental research and was a major driving force behind the Swedish Government's establishment of the Stockholm Prize in Criminology. With Heather Strang, he has also carried out a landmark series of 12 large-scale experiments in Australia and the UK on the effectiveness of restorative justice. He has also made a phenomenal contribution to the American Society of Criminology as lead guitarist and singer of The Hot Spots, his all-criminologist rock band!

Sherman has, deservedly, received many accolades, including the Presidency of the American Society of Criminology and the International Society of Criminology, the Edwin Sutherland Award of the American Society of Criminology and the Joan McCord Award of the Academy of Experimental Criminology. He is a man of prodigious energy and enthusiasm who has managed to carry out many experiments that most criminologists considered to be impossible. This reflects not only his towering intellect but also his remarkable optimism that everything is possible. When asked how on earth he managed to achieve so much, he suggested 'Don't ask for permission, ask for forgiveness'. Perhaps more path-breaking projects could be completed if more researchers adopted this courageous motto!

Professor L.W. Sherman with Dr R.K. Raghavan, former Director, Central Bureau of Investigation, India, International Conference on Evidence-Based Policing, 2008.

Chapter 3

Solid Science but No Ivory Tower:
The Institute's Teaching Programmes

Solid Science...

During the negotiations for the founding of an Institute of Criminology in Cambridge the University Grants Committee proposed that the functions of the Institute should place research as the primary objective, and that postgraduate instruction should be offered only 'if there is shown to be a need for it'. Radzinowicz (1988, p.21) regarded this as 'preposterous' and from the outset his vision included the first full-time postgraduate course in Criminology in the UK (there are now close to a hundred). So the creative tension between research and teaching, familiar to many academics, was there in the Institute's work from the very beginning.

In May 1966, Sir Leon described the purpose of the postgraduate course in the following way:

The course was not intended to provide professional training… [since] special instruction for this purpose was available in colleges and training centres. The original object of the Diploma course was [therefore] to impart a sound knowledge of criminology…; to form an aptitude for teaching and research…; and to train a critical mind towards basic problems of the administration of criminal justice.

(Quoted in Radzinowicz 1988, p.42)

The course at that time comprised seven key elements: the nature of crime and explanations of it; the study of people legally defined as criminal; the study of the impact of crime on society; the study of the criminal law in its broader social and political setting; the study of the processes of law enforcement; the analysis of the penal system, and of its alternatives; and studies of the evolution of penal legislation and penal policy. Criminology was seen as a 'composite' rather than as a simple discipline from the outset, and in a prescient comment Radzinowicz suggested that 'criminology (like crime) is a national product and therefore a variable one' (Radzinowicz 1988, pp.42–3). In this account, he did not draw attention to the distinctive nature of the Cambridge programme, but it is certainly arguable that there is one, for criminology 'Cambridge style' has always linked empirical research and theory, and there has always been a specific aim to help students examine problems and theories more objectively and scientifically.

Whilst it is hard to capture all the changes that have taken place over the years, we have gone from the Diploma in 1961 to an MPhil (beginning in 1977–8), and from five set courses and three-hour examination papers (with no dissertation) to two core courses (Criminological Theories and Criminological Research Methods) and three optional courses within four thematic areas: the causes of crime (developmental criminology, crime and its explanation and context, cross-cultural comparisons), experimental criminology and prevention (developmental prevention, situational prevention, and evidence-based policy and research); forensic mental health (mental health and crime, risk assessment and management, and forensic treatment) and criminal justice (the sociology of punishment, legal decision-making and sociology of prisons).

View from Clare Bridge to Garret Hostel Bridge.

The 18,000-word dissertation required of each MPhil student comprises a third of the whole degree and provides opportunity to demonstrate both theoretical concepts and methodological training through a small amount of empirical work. There are also now two MPhil progammes: the MPhil in Criminology (nine months) and the MPhil in Criminological Research (12 months) – reflecting the need to provide a distinctive route for prospective PhD students.

Moreover, the 'science' of criminology has become immeasurably more complex and sophisticated over time. From the days when the 'dark figure' of crime was itself a startling revelation and the 'self-report' survey an innovative mechanism to measure it, there is now a world-leading national survey (the British Crime Survey) much admired around the globe, the intricacies of which, alone, could fill an entire methods course. And questions as to 'realistic' evaluative research design have been overtaken by research infused with philosophical realism and notions of 'real world research', systematic field procedures are now accompanied by 'systematic reviews' of the literature, meta-analyses, and ever more sophisticated statistical analysis. Starting points in the 1960s were perhaps 'randomisation', 'multi-stage' and 'multi-phase' sampling techniques and statistical significance. Students in the 2000s contend with on-line surveys, computer interactive interviews, the use of video in ethnography and computer-assisted analysis of qualitative data, for instance, and quickly move on to discourse analysis, linear regression, factor, and path analysis as well as spatial analysis. The controversial debates of the day revolve around the role and use of randomised control trials (drawing on medicine); ethical dimensions of research, such as research involving on-line chat rooms; politics and policy and publications (for example, the perceived preference for particular types of methodologies within the Ministry of Justice, the search for evidence-based policy but the discomfort of this when research findings don't support political claims, and difficulties in finding new avenues for publication in a world driven by academic performance indicators). Thus the scope, complexity, and implications of research methodology have all changed, and the intensity of the Institute's training in this sphere reflects these changes. In-house training is supplemented by

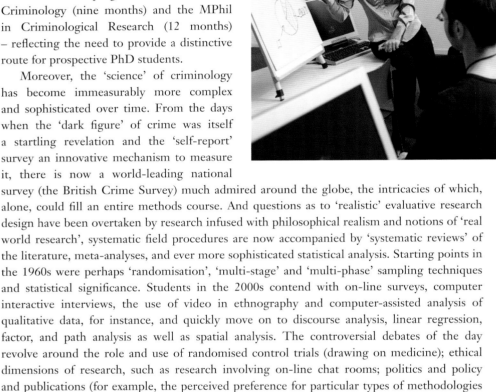

Dr Mandeep Dhami, Senior Lecturer in Criminology, teaching students.

I came to the Institute to study for my PhD in 2003. I chose the Institute because I was inspired by its work. The Prisons Research Centre, the Institute, and its many leading scholars provided a rich intellectual environment in which to undertake serious study and to develop academic expertise. In addition, the resources and staff at the Radzinowicz Library offered a level of support to PhD study that made my time there a positive and rewarding student experience.

Dr Deb Drake, Lecturer in Criminology at the Open University, UK participation in a 'joint schools' venture (a multi-departmental methods training course) which, for those students taking the MPhil in Criminological Research, involves a substantial part of the teaching timetable.

Teaching about criminological theories in the Institute in the 1960s was clearly exciting following the recognition of white collar crime, labelling theory, and early interest in victims. But it followed distinctive disciplinary tracks: sociology, psychiatry and psychology. Criminological theory in the 2000s is again more sophisticated and wide-ranging and is reflected in the blurring of disciplinary boundaries, so much so that there is an intergrated theories course. The content thus ranges from developmental and life course theories, rational choice theory, and modern theories of psychopathy, to late-modernity, crime and insecurity, realism, feminism, and post-modernism. Importantly, exposure to criminological theories goes beyond the core 'theories course' and the present structure of the MPhil programme facilitates this.

More generally, the full-time MPhil programme has changed to reflect the fact that many of our students now come with some previous criminological training from undergraduate programmes. (There are now over 900 undergraduate criminology courses – including joint honours courses – listed in UK universities alone). As always perhaps, students come especially from first degrees in Psychology, Sociology, Law, and Social Policy, but often now with a strong exposure to criminological ideas within these disciplines. However, it is not unknown for students to come from the Natural Sciences, History, Geography, Divinity, Medicine and English, for example, and with increasingly exotic combinations of first degrees – Criminology and Dance included. Students have applied for the MPhil programme from countries ranging from Australia to Zambia in recent years (see page 28), though numbers from the UK have declined since about 2000 (changes to funding arrangements and accumulated debts from undergraduate degrees no doubt playing their part, alongside the growth in postgraduate degrees in criminology at other institutions). We also witness fluctuations in numbers in line with other social science subjects, but the MPhil programme remains a central teaching programme in the Institute and is foundational to its other activities.

There have been other important developments in the full-time course along the way. What is now called 'Recognition' from the Economic and Social Research Council (ESRC) – marking the course out as one of the best places to study criminology, in view of its capacity to train future researchers – has been important. Whilst the Institute had enjoyed ESRC funding in the form of studentships for many years, Recognition was a major fillip and one which the Institute has worked hard to sustain. It currently brings with it four so-called '1+3' studentships (for the MPhil followed by three years funding for a PhD).

The foundational 'training' element in the Institute's MPhil teaching activity has been mirrored in the development of a PhD programme in recent years. The numbers of students doing a PhD at the Institute have increased enormously over the 50 year period, from a handful in the 1960s to nearly 40 in 2009. The days of two or three PhD students sharing an office have long gone; even in our purpose-built new building we are now contemplating bunk desks. Moreover, doing a PhD these days goes well beyond the production of 80,000 words reflecting an original contribution to knowledge. The Institute's PhD programme serves to provide general research training to equip students for an academic career (or variety of careers) as well. As part of the ESRC Recognition process in the 1990s the Institute developed a Training Support and Development Programme for PhD students which includes, alongside methodological training, a specific focus on Personal, Communication and Professional skills ('transferable skills'). The sessions revolve around students' ongoing work, discussion of contemporary challenges in theoretical criminology, new developments in research design and analysis, ethical issues, research management, and presentational skills amongst other things. One former PhD student reminds us that he learned an important 'transferable skills' lesson when, having arrived for a PhD party, and determined to be helpful, he opened every bottle of wine in sight and cut up twenty French loaves of bread...spending the late hours of the evening, long after the party, trying to offload it all!

Probation officers on the MSt (Penology) course, 2006.

Current PhD topics reflect wide intellectual interests: from religious communities and their effects in prisons, the power of forensic psychology within the British penal context, female serial murderers, ethnic identity and attitudes towards the police, police responses to diversity, drug-assisted sexual assault, mechanisms explaining intergenerational transmission of offending, formalised modelling of action theory in the explanation of crime, risk factors and delinquency, the development of police interview models, victims in the youth justice system, mental health courts, socio-emotional explanations for public punitiveness, crime in Northern Ireland, racism in the media, late modern probation practice, adolescents' experiences of criminal justice and the impact on their identity, the concept of care in prisons, and bullying in schools – to the effectiveness of restorative justice, the concept of order in prisons, restorative justice and community service in Chile, and power relations among prisoners and prison officers in Ukraine. Versatility and intellectual vibrancy are here in abundance!

Our MPhil and PhD students continue to go on to posts in the police, prison and probation, law, and clinical psychology, but also to research posts in the Ministry of Justice, management consultancy, research in social policy, media and marketing, non-governmental organisations, the prosecution service, and teaching posts in universities around the world, to name only some of their very varied destinations.

There was obvious tension in trying to create a balance between research and teaching in the early days of the Institute. That tension is still there, but it is for the most part a creative tension in which each informs the other. The MPhil programme and PhD programme are – as

It is no exaggeration to say that my MPhil year in 1990/1991 was a life-changing event. I was invigorated by my studies and the camaraderie with fellow students has led to enduring friendships around the globe. In 1998 I came back for more...the PhD was extremely hard work but also rewarding and enjoyable with the support of a good supervisor, other academics, and PhD students - not to mention the first-class facilities of the Radzinowicz Library. My PhD studies required me to adopt a rigorous analytical and critical approach to research. It is that discipline which I bring to my current role.

DR VICKY KEMP, PRINCIPAL CRIMINAL RESEARCHER IN THE LEGAL SERVICES RESEARCH CENTRE, UK

I came to the Institute in the autumn of 1968 fresh from New Zealand. I was in awe of the cosmopolitan and academic atmosphere of Cambridge. It was wonderful to study in that old house, in a small international group of students whom one could get to know well both personally and intellectually. We had very good times together, including visiting prisons as a group. I learnt how such real world experience provided a framework for academic study, which I have used successfully in my own teaching career. The course of my career is entirely connected to the people I met at the Institute; two professors affiliated with the Institute provided me with a job and a place in a PhD programme, respectively.

DR CAROL BOHMER, LECTURER, DARTMOUTH COLLEGE, USA

they always have been – essential components of the Institute's reputation for 'cutting-edge' teaching and research.

....but no ivory tower

Academic researchers, perhaps especially those working at the cutting edge of their field, are not always the best communicators when it comes to explaining their work either to the media or to politicians or even to those practising professionals who could most benefit from putting ideas into practice. But from its earliest beginnings, the Institute of Criminology collectively, and some of its academic staff individually, have aspired to build bridges between the academy and the practical world. The outstanding individual achievement in this respect has been the work of David Thomas. In the 1970s, his pioneering research work on the sentencing policy and practice of the Court of Appeal (Criminal Division) rapidly led to invitations to participate in conferences and then training for judges in this sphere of work. That in turn led to the development of key practice-oriented texts on sentencing, continuing work on judicial training over many years, and the warm respect of many judges and legal practitioners, exemplified in the generous tribute from the present Lord Chief Justice on page 52.

Collectively, the Institute from the outset recognised that professions such as the police, the prison service and the probation service have their own in-service training, and that there should be no attempt to trespass on these. But, thought Leon Radzinowicz, there was also a 'clear need' for a different type of course for such professionals: 'It should aim at broadening the outlook of those attending, at showing them something of the relevance of research to their work, and at bringing them up to date with the most recent research findings. It should raise them above and beyond their individual (however valuable yet necessarily restricted) experiences and stimulate them to reflect upon big issues, dominant trends, or shifts of emphasis, in the concerns of criminal justice' (Radzinowicz 1988, p.73).

Those objectives have remained central to the activities of the Institute ever since, although the target audiences have varied from time to time as have the type and nature of the courses and events designed to deliver them. It is, of course, one thing to entertain such lofty ideals, but it is another to realise them. A visit to the archives bears testimony to the delicacies which have to be observed if the sensitivities of judges, the ambitions of politicians, the concerns for confidentiality of civil servants, let alone the *amour propre* of academics are not to be offended as the details of syllabuses and methods of teaching are worked out, and then evaluated after the event. But it has been a two-way street as what would now be called customers and providers reached some form of compromise about what customers thought providers should provide and what providers thought customers needed.

David Thomas, drawing by John Edwards, reproduced by permission of the Master and Fellows of Trinity Hall.

David Thomas

David Thomas is the most improbable revolutionary you could ever meet. Yet he has revolutionised the approach of the courts in this country to sentencing. It has been a remarkable achievement, the product of an intensely inquiring mind, close and meticulous analysis of impenetrable statutory language, all accompanied by lively wit and warm good humour. That perhaps is why you will never find a judge who takes the slightest umbrage at anything David says or writes. To the contrary, we want to hear and read him.

A casual glance at the Criminal Appeal Reports in the early 1970s will demonstrate that there was very little interest in appeals against sentence, and even less access to them. It was possible to deduce some desultory basic principles out of which David managed to produce the appearance of consistency and coherence in his book, *Principles of Sentencing in the Court of Appeal* (1970). I still have my own copy, unfortunately of the second edition. As I look at it, what strikes me is how slim a volume it is. Before that volume, and for some time afterwards, there was nothing practical. We all knew that the entitlement of the state to impose punishment, and the true objectives of sentencing, and similar questions had provoked profound intellectual and philosophical discussions. But for the sentencing decision itself, we relied on judicial common sense and experience. There was no structure; no real consistency of approach; no legislative interest.

David's life's work has been to illuminate the way in which sentencing process works in practice and, to the extent that the legislative torrent permits, to make it logical and coherent and consistent. Sentencing can never be a bureaucratic process, nor indeed can it ever be scientific, if only because in the end every crime is specific and the defendant is a human being with his own strengths and weaknesses, which fall to be considered in the sentencing decision. In other words, in what seems to me to be the most difficult of all judicial responsibilities – the sentencing of a fellow human being – David has strived to ensure that justice should be done according to law, equally and fairly in the sentencing decisions up and down the country.

David was perhaps born with an inherent sense about the workings of most judicial minds and the art of influencing them. He has never attempted to tell us how we should perform our responsibilities, but he has supplied us with the information which enables us better to address them. What he has done is to enable all those individual judgments, and there are many tens of thousands of them annually, to be fully informed.

We have been, and we continue to be, immensely advantaged by publications for which David is responsible. He is the Editor of *Current Sentencing Practice*, the vast four-volume encyclopaedia which has replaced his single slim volume from the 1960s; *The Criminal Appeal Reports (Sentencing)*, two volumes annually, covering literally hundreds of pages; the Editor of the Sentencing Cases noted monthly in the *Criminal Law Review*; the Sentencing Editor of *Archbold*; author of the *Sentencing Referencer*, and a regular contributor to numerous other publications. It is why his studies of proposed legislative changes have entertained, and no less than entertained, alarmed, what can fairly be described now as generations of judges and recorders. It is why so much legislation subjected to fair criticism by him before enactment is so often amended because it is unworkable in precisely the way he forecast. It is why he commands the admiration, respect and affection of the judiciary and the legal professions and why the grant to him of the accolade of honorary silk in 1996 was greeted with enthusiastic acclaim.

The legal establishment, supposedly so double-dyed conservative in its attitudes, was greeting the quiet revolutionary who had contributed so positively to the administration of justice, and applauding the overdue public recognition of that contribution.

Sir Igor Judge – Lord Chief Justice of England and Wales

The MSt in Applied Criminology and Police Management provided a rare opportunity for practical policing to juxtapose with contemporary debates in criminology. As a senior police officer with a strong operational background, the course provided me with an excellent opportunity to interact and debate with academic researchers and other professionals from the Criminal Justice System in a way that allowed me innovative reflection on contemporary issues of crime and justice. It certainly helped me to think more broadly about the complexity of policing.

PETER SHERIDAN, CHIEF EXECUTIVE OF COOPERATION IRELAND AND
A FORMER ASSISTANT CHIEF CONSTABLE IN THE POLICE SERVICE OF NORTHERN IRELAND

The earliest venture into this area was what Radzinowicz originally called the Advanced Course in Criminology but which soon became more generally known as the Senior Course. This first took place over four weeks in July and August 1960 with 45 carefully selected participants from the police, prison, probation and children's services together with prison doctors and psychologists, and magistrates and justices' clerks. But by all accounts the syllabus (see Radzinowicz 1988, appendix 13) was far too wide, the required reading too extensive, and the timetable too intensive to give sufficient scope for thinking time or audience participation. By 1966 after much feedback and some experimentation a newer, more streamlined formula, in which small group seminars formed the basis of teaching and course materials were distributed in advance, provided the basis for many subsequent and highly successful senior courses, since 1976 under the direction of David Farrington. The number of study weeks was reduced first

Examination questions for the fourth Diploma in Criminology course, 1965.

Appendix 9

AN EXAMPLE OF THE EXAMINATION FOR A DIPLOMA OF THE POST-GRADUATE COURSE IN CRIMINOLOGY

Diploma in Criminology, Examination Papers, 1965

Paper 1.   **CRIMINOLOGICAL THEORY AND SOCIOLOGY OF CRIME**

Answer *four* questions and no more

1. Assess the role of Gabriel Tarde in the development of criminological thought.
2. What lessons concerning the causation of crime may be learned from the study of persistent offenders?
3. "The study of the born criminal has died a natural death." Discuss.
4. Which criminological theory provides the best explanation for recent developments in teenage crime in Britain? Give your reasons.
5. Under what conditions is "organised crime" likely to flourish?
6. How far, in studying crimes against the person, is it profitable for the criminologist to have regard to the role of the victim?
7. Discuss the view that the person who commits a serious motoring offence may be just as "criminal" as other offenders against persons or property.
8. "Society carries within itself, in some sense, the seeds of all the crimes which are going to be committed" (QUETELET). Discuss.

Paper 2.   **PSYCHIATRIC AND PSYCHOLOGICAL ASPECTS OF CRIMINAL BEHAVIOUR**

Answer *four* questions and no more

1. Discuss critically the evidence for the theory that brain damage sustained before or during birth, even though it produces no permanent physical symptoms, may be the cause of the disturbed behaviour of some young persons.
2. What is the relevance to criminology of the theory of critical periods of learning?
3. What is known about the crime patterns and psychological make-up of individuals convicted of "indecent exposure"?

148

4. What social, psychological, and psychiatric characteristics are commonly found among murderers in England?
5. Contrast the interpretations and methods of treatment of a compulsive shoplifter given by (i) a psycho-analyst, and (ii) a behaviour therapist.
6. In the disposal of mentally abnormal offenders by the Courts, discuss the respective merits of (i) a Hospital Order, and (ii) a requirement of medical treatment under a Probation Order.
7. How far is it possible and desirable to "individualise" treatment in penal institutions? Illustrate your argument in relation to prisons, or borstals or approved schools.
8. What do you understand by "the therapeutic community" and what relevance does this approach have for institutional treatment of offenders?

Paper 3.   **METHODS OF CRIMINOLOGICAL RESEARCH**

Answer *four* questions and no more

1. What can be done about the problem of "non-response" in criminological research?
2. How far is it true to say that the design of interview schedules and the techniques of interviewing in criminological research are substantially different from those in other social research?
3. What is meant by "randomisation"? Illustrate this principle with reference to any examples of research into the results of treatment.
4. To what extent are the present *Criminal Statistics* useful for different kinds of criminological research? How could they be made more valuable for research purposes?
5. "The creation of a realistic design of evaluative research would unquestionably do more to speed the development of a science of penology than any other single contribution." Discuss this statement.
6. "That young sciences should be much concerned with classification is normal enough; and the social sciences are no exception" (BARBARA WOOTTON). Discuss this statement in relation to research on offences and offenders.
7. Distinguish between a "multi-stage" sample and a "multi-phase" sample. Indicate the usefulness of each for the design of samples in criminology.
8. Do you accept that there is "an ideological gulf separating those persons responsible for treatment from those responsible for treatment evaluation"? If so, how can these differences be resolved?

149

to three and finally to two, and in its final format the course participants were grouped into committees charged with working through problems defined in the seminars with light-touch guidance from staff members. Each committee then reported their findings to the whole class. Over the years the constituency for the course widened to include judges, magistrates, youth justice workers and crime prevention coordinators as well as representatives from leading NGOs. Indeed the great benefit of the Senior Course, appreciated by virtually all participants was the way in which members began to appreciate criminal justice from the perspective of workers in other agencies. This was facilitated by sessions in which participants were invited to describe and evaluate the functions and problems of their own agencies which became a regular feature of the course. In a real sense the Institute had foreshadowed the idea of multi-agency cooperation long before it had become a mantra in criminal justice. The last Senior Course took place in 2004, however, perhaps because multi-agency working had become, to some degree, a reality and it was no longer necessary to come to Cambridge for that experience.

At about the same time as the new formula for the Senior Course was introduced, a philanthropic foundation, which initially wanted to remain anonymous but was subsequently happy to be identified as the Barrow and Geraldine S. Cadbury Trust, offered funding for what came to be called the Cropwood Fellowships – named after one of the Cadbury family houses. These short-term Fellowships were intended to enable practitioners in the field of criminal justice and the treatment of offenders to spend a period of between three weeks and six months to pursue an approved project of research or study at the Institute where they would be free from their normal duties. It was this freedom from the exigent day and the opportunity it provided for daily informal contact with members of the research community which Cropwood Fellows, and indeed virtually all practitioner participants on the Senior Course and later courses, have found so valuable. People in stressful jobs at the coalface of criminal justice rarely have time to sit and reflect upon the wider context within which they work. Between 1968 and 2003 some 129 Fellowships were awarded, about 70% of which were to members of the Police or

Archbishop of York, the Rt Revd Dr John Sentamu, visiting the Institute in February 2008.

As a part of my studies I conducted research into the use of the anti-social behaviour order (ASBO) which, with Senior Research Fellow, Elizabeth Burney as co-author, was later published by the Howard League for Penal Reform as The ASBO: Wrong Turning, Dead End. *As a serving police officer I had experience of the use of these orders and over time I had become concerned about their increased use, their long-term effects and the conditions imposed under them. In my research I examined those cases where the legislation had been abused and the orders were not used effectively. I also explored what the possible long-term effects of these orders could be and whether they might in fact be criminalising people.*

One of my concerns was the possibility that ASBOs may lead to a longer criminal career. My book received widespread publicity and was influential in a re-examination of the use of these orders. As a result of this work, I was invited back to the Institute on 21 February 2008 as one of a small group of speakers on the visit of Rt Revd Dr John Sentamu, Archbishop of York.

NEIL WAIN, CHIEF SUPERINTENDENT, GREATER MANCHESTER POLICE, MASTER OF STUDIES IN APPLIED CRIMINOLOGY AND POLICE MANAGEMENT, 2007

The Institute MPhil team during a football tournament, 2006.

Probation Services or representatives from the Courts or Legal Services. The remainder were divided between psychologists, medical practitioners including psychiatrists, social workers, teachers and persons working for non-governmental organisations. The topics pursued usually related closely to the fields from which the Fellows were drawn but ranged from police juvenile liaison schemes to an annotated bibliography of the mafia, via studies of maternal homicide, meter theft, and of the treatment of mentally abnormal offenders. The studies often resulted either in published papers or reports used internally in the agencies concerned. Particularly noteworthy from the early days of the scheme was Fred Jarvis' *Probation Officers' Manual* published by Butterworth in 1969, but there have been many others which continue to play an influential role in their respective fields. Alongside the Cropwood Fellowships the Institute developed a series of Cropwood Round-Table Conferences which served the need to consider emerging topics of pressing importance to the criminal justice community where a smallish group of well qualified and potentially influential participants could exchange views with academics with a view to reaching at least preliminary conclusions on the matters at hand. The last Cropwood Fellowships were awarded in 2003, and the most recent Cropwood Conference was held in 2007. At the time of writing an evaluation of the strengths and weaknesses of the Cropwood programme is under way, so that the Institute and Trust can consider the future of the scheme (see chapter 10). Other occasional conferences and regular seminars also bring academics and practitioners together on matters of mutual interest, with practitioners being consulted on research plans and academics advising on practical implications. Such contacts have become part of the warp and weft of the Institute's criminal justice cloth.

Radzinowicz explicitly rejected the idea that bridge-building courses should lead to any examination or degree, and he believed that they should not be convened too frequently. The Senior Course was delivered on a biennial basis and participants were well content at having their attendance listed on their CVs – the chances of selection in any given year quickly fell to about one in ten – even though no formal qualification resulted. All this began to change in the mid-1990s after Peter Ryan, then the National Director of Police Training, had approached Tony Bottoms, then Director of the Institute, to explore whether Cambridge would take a lead role in the training of potential Chief Constables and Assistant Chief Constables in partnership with the National Directorate. It was agreed that Institute staff would teach for an initial four weeks a year as part of the Strategic Command Course (SCC) at Bramshill National Police Staff College, after which participants would be invited – and recommended by the National Directorate – to attend two further weeks of training in Cambridge. Subject to satisfactory assessment of written assignments this six weeks of training would lead to the award of a Diploma through the University's Board of Continuing Education (now the Institute of Continuing Education). Successful candidates could, if they wished, continue their studies for a further year, on a part-time basis organised around study blocks in Cambridge, and during which they would submit a substantial dissertation in part-fulfilment of the requirements for the then brand-new Cambridge Master of Studies Degree. As a matter of diplomatic convenience, the first year's (Diploma) work was described as training rather than education, but the 'educational' aspect of Radzinowicz's original vision was emphatically not breached.

The Diploma/MSt programme, being initially linked to the SCC, was aimed at serving officers at the rank of Superintendent or Chief Superintendent, with high potential. Hence, of

MPhil students at a seminar given by Professor Wikström.

A 'busman's holiday' for four students on the MSt course in June 2004. Returning to their rooms at Homerton College, three senior policemen and one FBI agent rescued a teenager from a violent assault. Two of the attackers were caught by Chief Superintendent Mark Hopkins and Chief Superintendent Adrian Leppard. Almost as frightened as the victim was the junior police officer called to take the perpetrators into custody under such high-ranking scrutiny.

www.cambridge-news.co.uk/news   EVENING NEWS, FRIDAY

Total of 12 years for pair who attacked student

Ferocious attack: Above left, Aaron Tonner and above right, Christopher Tonner were convicted of robbing Cambridge student George Schooling. Police chiefs Mark Hopkins far left, and Adrian Leppard left, were passing at the time of the offence and helped apprehend the pair.

Brothers Grim jailed

A PAIR of vicious brothers have been jailed for a total of 12 years

Father-of-two Christo Tillyard Way, Cambridge has a string of previous

www.cambridge-news.co.uk/news   EVENING NEWS, THURSDAY, MARCH 3, 2005   11

Police officers and an FBI agent to the rescue of disabled man

those who have graduated with at least a Diploma (and many found that operational duties did not permit them to return for a second year), more than 75 went on to become Assistant Chief Constables, more than 25 Deputy Chief Constables and more than 30 became Chief Constables. But in the early 2000s, the Home Office drastically shortened the SCC, and in consequence the Cambridge input to that course (and, with it, the link to Diploma teaching) had to be discontinued. Having gained much valuable experience in this kind of teaching, the Institute decided to attempt to recruit for the Diploma and MSt on a 'stand-alone' basis, with a slightly wider recruitment base so far as police ranks were concerned. Initially, as was to be expected, there was a sharp drop in numbers. However, after a few years, recruitment is now above its previous level, notably aided by, in the transitional years, a strong contingent of officers from the Police Service of Northern Ireland as well as officers from Trinidad and Tobago.

In order to ensure that the content of the Diploma/MSt programme in Applied Criminology and Management (Police Studies) meets police educational needs, the successive Course Directors have maintained close consultation with those responsible for police training – initially at the National Directorate, then Centrex and now the National Policing Improvement Agency (NPIA). Interestingly, the first Director of NPIA, Peter Neyroud, is himself a former prize-winning graduate of the course. (The prize in question was established by the family of Victor Lissack in memory of his work at the criminal bar, and Neyroud was the first of 15 recipients so far of the Victor Lissack Award – see chapter 12). The present Director of the Course, Lawrence Sherman, has negotiated a series of bursaries with the NPIA and is redeveloping the course as a Police Executive Programme with a strong focus on evidence-based policing. Indeed, the 2008 cohort were able to benefit from attending a highly successful International Conference on Evidence-Based Policing which was held in Cambridge and which is likely to become an annual event.

Professor Roy King presenting the prize for the best MSt (Penology) thesis to Nicky Marfleet, deputy governor of Pentonville Prison, in the gardens at Fitzwilliam College, 2008.

The final strand in this rather intricate series of formal links with criminal justice practitioners is the Diploma and MSt in Applied Criminology, Penology and Management. This had its origins as the MSt in Applied Criminology and Management (Prison Studies) which was established in 1998 following discussions between senior officials in the Prison Service, and, for the Institute, Tony Bottoms and Alison Liebling, about the need for greater management expertise as well as criminological understanding among senior prison managers. Not surprisingly it followed closely the model successfully developed for the MSt in Police Studies, while also drawing upon the management expertise from members of the University's Judge Institute of Management Studies, which was a partner in the original contract. The programme was fully funded by the Prison Service and it continued to enjoy the support of Senior Course alumnus Martin Narey in his successive roles as Director General of the Prison Service, Commissioner for Corrections and Director General of the National Offender Management Service (NOMS). As NOMS became a reality so the course was extended to include senior probation staff under its present title but in a difficult funding climate the contract came to an end in 2006. Without guaranteed central funding the course has, like the police course, continued as a free-standing fee-paying course and has developed its recruitment base both internationally – with members from the United States, Bangladesh, Brazil, Spain and Trinidad and Tobago – and by widening the areas of criminal justice from which participants are drawn. The course now has members who work in both public and private sector prisons, and in NOMS headquarters, as well as the magistracy together with a number of lawyers and psychologists with a critical interest in the criminal justice field. Whilst management and managerialism remain strong components of the course this is now dealt with wholly within house.

When Tony Bottoms gave an introductory speech at the formal launch of the MSt (Prison Studies) he developed an extended metaphor by likening the management of prisons to the running of a long-haul airline – time-consuming reception and check-in procedures, concerns about safety, the fear of first timers and the blasé approach of frequent fliers and recidivists, the importance of food in an otherwise somewhat sterile environment, concern about the allocation of neighbours and cellmates, the eventual disembarkation and discharge and picking up one's life after a period in suspension. Perhaps, by way of conclusion, it is worth extending this metaphor: if the MSt and similar programmes constitute a journey in which academics and practitioners are brought into regular close contact as travelling companions, it is a journey in which, by common consent, both parties seem to benefit in equal measure.

But what of the future? Can this joint journey be extended? The recent strength of the MSt programmes shows the enormous interest in criminological research, properly presented, among criminal justice officials internationally. That interest is based primarily on the value that basic and applied research can have for improving the millions of decisions made daily about crimes, victims, suspects, and convicted offenders. Yet the body of research evidence is growing more slowly than the professional and executive appetite for such evidence. At the same time, MSt students seek the Institute's guidance about how to re-shape the governmental and political context to make research a more important consideration in making decisions. One possibility for linking these issues more closely would be the development of research networks in relation to MSt courses, so that agencies and research bodies would fund mid-career executive students to become research managers and liaison officers for university research projects, and this kind of model is currently being debated. How the debate will conclude, no-one can know at present. But the very fact that the debate is taking place is evidence of the enormous strides that have been made.

I came to Cambridge from Ghana in 2004 for my MPhil degree. Studying in Cambridge has been a unique experience, and marks a stark contrast with life at my former university. The quality of teaching and supervision was and still remains world-class, with excellent resources and support from academic and administrative staff, and my colleagues. Little things like calling a professor by his or her first name were a cultural shock to me, having come from a university where student-lecturer interactions often mirrored that of a master-servant relationship. Here at the Institute, it's fine to have your own ideas, as long as you can defend them! Fortunately for me, I received further funding from the Lopez-Rey Fund, the Cambridge Commonwealth Trust and St Edmund's College for my doctoral research on police legitimacy in Ghana. The unique academic environment at the Institute made my student years truly pleasant and memorable, and I learned so much.

Dr Justice Tankebe, British Academy Postdoctoral Research Fellow, Institute of Criminology, University of Cambridge, and Research Fellow of Fitzwilliam College

Chapter 4

Forensic Psychiatry and Criminology: A Special Collaboration

Criminology in Britain developed from a tradition of applied medico-legal and psychiatric practice that had become established in prisons and hospitals from the 1860s onwards. In the early decades of the 20th century the major British scientific publications on crime were written by doctors trained in psychiatry and working in prisons, and the first university lectures in 'Criminology' were given to postgraduate medical students in Birmingham in 1921–2 (see Garland 1988).

Despite these origins, in most contemporary universities criminology and forensic psychiatry are studied and taught in different departments. It has therefore been an important and special feature of the work of the Institute of Criminology that, throughout its history, it has included a psychiatrist among its established staff. This policy was integral to Leon Radzinowicz's interdisciplinary vision for the Institute of Criminology (see chapter 1), and, in consequence, one of the first senior staff appointed to the Institute in 1960 was Donald West, who had trained in psychiatry in London under Sir Aubrey Lewis, Frederick Kraupl-Taylor, and Peter Scott, one of the leading forensic psychiatrists of the time.

Donald West's contributions to the Institute's research programme, and to its teaching, were substantial and enduring. His far-sighted longitudinal study, the Cambridge Study in Delinquent Development, is discussed in the next chapter. His first published research report while at the Institute was *The Habitual Prisoner* (1963), a clinical and social study of recidivist offenders and men sentenced to preventive detention. This was followed by a study of homicide cases, *Murder Followed by Suicide* (1965), based on medical records, and then *The Young Offender* (1967), a comprehensive review of evidence about the extent, causation and management of criminal behaviour by young people. These studies were characterised by careful and detailed clinical assessments, analyses of research evidence, and judicious drawing of inferences in restrained, lucid prose. Although the writing style was neutral and understated, the messages conveyed were powerful – countering unsubstantiated beliefs and highlighting concern for the humanity and welfare of offenders. *The Habitual Prisoner* concluded that the most dangerous and violent criminals were unlikely to be found amongst the men who were repeatedly imprisoned or sentenced to preventive detention: the habitual prisoners were more likely to have repeated histories of social failure and psychiatric difficulties. *Murder Followed by Suicide* reported the remarkably high rates of self-inflicted death after tragic inter-personal and family homicides, and the significant number of killings of infants by suicidal mothers experiencing depressive illness. The final chapter of *The Young Offender* (characteristically entitled 'Some Cautionary Afterthoughts'), written 40 years ago, noted how the research evidence of the time showed that in spite of the publicity given to notorious crimes,

> ...the fact is that the great majority of the offences committed by young persons are not very serious, not carefully planned or premeditated, and not part of a professional commitment to crime.
>
> (WEST 1967, P.291)

The Ten Commandments. *This work was painted by an inmate of HMP and YOI Guys Marsh and was Highly Commended at the Koestler Awards, 2006. It was bought for the Radzinowicz Library through the Koestler Trust for Arts Inside.*

There was, however, a minority of very persistent young offenders whose histories were characterised by multiple social deprivations and whose persistent delinquency could not be satisfactorily accounted for by biological, psychological, environmental or sociological theories alone. There were no single explanations or remedies:

> *Nobody expects any one explanation or treatment method to solve all health problems. Advocates of a single cure-all for delinquency, whether it is harsher punishment or more child guidance, are equally unrealistic. An unremitting attack on a wide front, using different methods for different problems, holds out the best hope for progress. Above all, social and penal measures, which seek to change behaviour, should be securely based on rational inquiry into the causal factors involved, and should include objective assessment of the results of different courses of action.*

(WEST 1967, PP.298–9)

The Bethlem Hospital, 19th-century print. Parts of this building survive as the Imperial War Museum but the Hospital itself moved to its present site in Bromley in 1930. The birthplace of British psychiatry and the first charitable mental hospital, the Bethlem Hospital amalgamated with the Maudsley in 1948 to form a single postgraduate psychiatric teaching hospital. Both Donald West and Adrian Grounds trained at the Maudsley.

Donald West's later work focussed especially on research into sex offences and sexuality: for example *Understanding Sexual Attacks* (1978), *Sexual Victimisation* (1985), and *Children's Sexual Encounters with Adults* (1990). These built on his early (1955) and influential book on homosexuality (see chapter 2).

Donald West had been, in University language, a 'non-clinical post-holder', although in fact he continued to see a few patients to maintain his clinical skills. After his retirement in 1984, arrangements were made to constitute the Institute's academic post in psychiatry similarly to other clinical academic posts in the University, so that the teaching post would be linked with an honorary National Health Service contract to provide a substantive, part-time clinical service in forensic psychiatry for the local community. The person appointed to this post was Adrian Grounds, whose work has therefore been divided between the University and NHS, an arrangement that ensures continuing engagement in casework and active professional links with health and criminal justice agencies.

Collaborative research conducted by Adrian Grounds over the last two decades has included a study of access to mental health services by remanded prisoners with mental illness, and a national study of access to medium-secure psychiatric units. Both studies indicated the slow and highly selective gate-keeping procedures that can impede admission to mental health services. More recent and ongoing research has focused on understanding the psychological and social consequences of wrongful conviction and imprisonment, based on in-depth psychiatric assessments of people who have served long-term prison sentences after being wrongfully convicted (Grounds 2005). Evidence was found of severe traumatic effects including personality change, post-traumatic stress disorder, a loss of practical skills and lasting difficulties with adapting to life after release. Besides highlighting the tragedy of wrongful conviction, the study indicates the need for much more thorough and sensitive research enquiries into the longitudinal effects of imprisonment on the psychological lives, attachments and adjustment of prisoners and their families.

A wide range of doctoral theses on psychiatric aspects of criminology has also been completed by research students, on topics ranging from the relation between architecture and therapeutic aims in secure units, public attitudes towards mentally disordered offenders, relationships between mental illness and culpability, motivation for treatment amongst sex offenders, and discretionary decision making by tribunals and courts in psychiatric cases.

Adrian Grounds

Adrian Grounds qualified in medicine from the University of Nottingham. After house officer posts in medicine, neurosurgery and neurology, he trained in psychiatry at the Maudsley Hospital London. He then undertook specialist training in forensic psychiatry at the Maudsley and Bethlem Royal Hospitals, and Broadmoor Hospital. Between 1984 and 1987 he was a clinical lecturer at the Institute of Psychiatry, London. He completed his DM in 1986, a study of transfers of sentenced prisoners to Broadmoor Hospital under the Mental Health Act. He was elected a Fellow of the Royal College of Psychiatrists in 1996.

He moved to the Institute of Criminology in 1987 as a University Lecturer, with additional NHS clinical responsibilities as a consultant forensic psychiatrist. His research interests have been in the service needs of offenders with mental disorders, and more recently on the psychiatric and psychological consequences of wrongful conviction and imprisonment. In his NHS work he has contributed to substantial developments in forensic mental health services in Cambridgeshire, and during recent years has been a member of Cambridgeshire's MAPPA (Multi-Agency Public Protection Arrangements) Strategic Management Board. In 1998 he was appointed as one of the Sentence Review Commissioners responsible for implementing the provisions for the early release of paramilitary prisoners in Northern Ireland following the Good Friday Agreement. He is also one of the Parole Commissioners in Northern Ireland, and a Trustee of the Prison Reform Trust.

Adrian Grounds,
Senior Lecturer at the
Institute and Consultant
Forensic Psychiatrist at
Addenbrookes Hospital.

When Donald West set out the justifications for maintaining the clinical approach within criminology nearly 30 years ago (West 1980) he argued that individual and social explanations of offending are not incompatible, that immersion in casework is likely to sharpen rather than reduce awareness of relationships between politics, social injustice and crime, and that the evaluation of treatment studies must be based on sound methodological understanding. He also emphasised the existence of high rates of psychiatric morbidity in offender populations, a matter of compelling practical importance that remains painfully evident. Indeed, he had noted in 1967 that,

> *... doctors have a regrettable propensity to reject offenders of all ages if their defects are too trouble-some or apparently unchangeable, and to cast them out of medical care into penal custody, as once lepers were cast untreated into colonies.*

(WEST 1967, P.297)

Forty years on, it is a sentiment still commonly echoed by criminal justice practitioners.

The importance of clinical and psychiatric contributions to criminology has become greater and more multi-faceted in the contemporary era. New developments raise pressing questions. For example, the contributions of psychology and psychiatry to the growing dominance of risk assessment and management in penal policy need to be critically understood. Questions have also arisen about the relationship between mental ill health and failures of due process in the context of detention. More generally, criminology can draw on major methodological and theoretical advances in clinical medicine, in fields ranging from the neurosciences to epidemiology to the conduct of randomised controlled trials.

Engagement with clinical work can also contribute to criminological insight. Casework constantly reveals contrasts between over-generalised explanatory theories of offending and the complexity and variety of offenders' individual lives. Central to criminology is human suffering. Offending causes suffering, victims experience suffering, and the penal system imposes suffering on offenders. The task for academic and practitioner alike in each domain is to seek to understand and minimise it.

from motor vehicles, shoplifting, theft from machines, assault, drug use and vandalism), which account for the majority of all conviction offences. However, only 29% had been convicted for one of these offences during the same age ranges (Farrington 1989).

Risk Factors, Mechanisms and Processes

We found that certain risk factors predict a high probability of offending. To illustrate this, we will concentrate on risk factors measured in childhood, at age 8–10, that predict convictions up to age 50 (see Farrington et al. 2009b).

The strongest family predictors were having a convicted parent or a delinquent sibling, poor parental supervision, and coming from a disrupted family (separation from a biological parent). The strongest individual predictors were low school attainment, high daring, poor concentration, and low non-verbal intelligence. The strongest behavioural predictors were troublesomeness (rated by peers and teachers) and dishonesty (rated by peers).

The most important independent predictors at age 8–10 were: a convicted parent, high daring, low school attainment, poor housing, a disrupted family and large family size. A simple risk score was developed by scoring each boy from 0 to 6 according to the number of these six risk factors that he possessed at age 8–10. Whereas only about 20% of those with none of these risk factors were convicted, over 80% of those with 4 or more risk factors were convicted. However, this is a retrospective prediction exercise. Just using one prospective predictor (troublesomeness), the percentage convicted increased from 22% of those who were low to 64% of those who were high at age 8–10. This gives a better indication of the true extent to which convictions can be predicted from childhood.

We have made several attempts to go beyond the identification of risk factors to test alternative theories about mechanisms and processes relating risk factors to offending. For example, we tested different explanations of the relationship between disrupted families (broken homes) and delinquency and found that, while boys from broken homes (permanently disrupted families) were more delinquent than boys from intact homes, they were not more delinquent than boys from intact high conflict families. Therefore, the loss of a parent was not the key factor. Overall, the most important factor was what happened after the family break. Boys who remained with their mother after the separation had the same delinquency rate as boys from intact low conflict families. Boys who remained with their father, with relatives or with others (eg foster parents) had high delinquency rates. Therefore, it was not true that broken homes always had undesirable consequences (Juby and Farrington 2001).

Life Events and Protective Factors

In a longitudinal survey, it is possible to investigate the effects of specific life events on the development of delinquency, by comparing before and after measures of offending. For example, the effects on delinquent behaviour of being found guilty in court were studied. If convictions have a deterrent or reformative effect, a boy's delinquent behaviour should decline after he is convicted. On the other hand, if convictions have stigmatising or contaminating effects, a boy's delinquent behaviour should increase after he is convicted. These hypotheses were tested by studying self-reports of delinquency before and after a boy was first convicted. The results suggested that first convictions had undesirable delinquency-amplifying effects.

Another investigation of the effect of a specific event on offending focused on unemployment. The key question was whether the boys committed more offences (according to official records) during their periods of unemployment than during their periods of employment. The results showed that the boys did indeed commit more crimes while unemployed than while employed. Furthermore, the difference was restricted to offences involving financial gain, such as theft, burglary, robbery, and fraud. There was no effect of unemployment on other offences, such as violence, vandalism, and drug use. These results suggest that the boys committed more offences while they were unemployed primarily because they lacked money at these times and were trying to get money (Farrington et al. 1986).

An important life event that encouraged desistance was moving out of London. Most families who moved out were upwardly mobile families who were moving to prosperous suburban areas in the Home Counties, often buying their own houses rather than renting in London. It was clear that both the official and self-reported offending of the men decreased after they or their families moved out of London, possibly because of the effect of the move in breaking up delinquent peer groups.

It is often believed that marriage is one of the best treatments for male offending. When we asked the males in their 20s why they had stopped offending, they often mentioned marriage and the influence of women, as well as the fact that they did not hang around so much with delinquent friends. Before-and-after analyses showed that getting married led to a decrease in conviction rates compared with remaining single, whereas separation from a wife led to an increase in conviction rates compared with staying married (Farrington and West 1995).

Life Success

We looked at life success amongst our sample group at ages 32 and 48, measured on nine criteria, including their employment and accommodation histories, cohabitation, alcohol and drug use, convictions and self-reported offending, anxiety/depression and violence. The vast majority were rated as successful at 32 and this improved further by 48 (Farrington et al. 2006).

The convicted men were divided into 47 desisters who were convicted only before age 21, 31 late-comers to crime who were convicted only at age 21 or older, and 65 persisters who were convicted both before and after age 21. The key question that was addressed is to what extent these categories of offenders were successful in different aspects of their lives at age 48. The good news is that the majority of all groups were considered to be leading successful lives: 95% of unconvicted men, 96% of desisters, 84% of late onset offenders, and 65% of persisters.

The most important finding is that desisters were not significantly different from unconvicted men in eight out of nine areas or in their total success score. Therefore, as with smoking, those who give up offending eventually become similar to non-offenders.

Late onset offenders were significantly different from unconvicted men in their alcohol and drug use. Interestingly, among the best predictors of late onset offenders were nervousness and having few friends at age 8–10, teacher-rated anxiety at age 12–14, high neuroticism at age 16 and not having had sexual intercourse by age 18. It seems that the protective effects of social inhibition in adolescence may wear off after age 21 when men leave home (Zara and Farrington 2009).

Policy Implications

The main policy implications of the Cambridge Study are relevant to risk assessment and risk-focused prevention. Risk assessment tools such as the EARL-20B (Early Assessment Risk List for Boys), which aims to identify children who are at risk of reoffending, are based on longitudinal

Revan. *Part of the Library's collection of art by prisoners, this was painted by an inmate of HMYOI Portland in 2005. It won a Merit Award in the Koestler Awards for 2005.*

surveys such as the Cambridge Study that have discovered the most important risk factors for offending. While risk assessment and risk-focused prevention are relevant to the onset and persistence of offending, the Cambridge Study also has policy implications for desistance (eg in showing the beneficial effects of employment, marriage and moving house).

Risk-focused prevention suggests that, in order to reduce offending, the key risk factors should be identified and programmes should be implemented to tackle these risk factors. Based on the Cambridge Study, it might be suggested that early prevention experiments are especially needed that target four important risk factors: low school attainment, poor parental child-rearing behaviour, impulsiveness and poverty.

Because of the link between offending and numerous other social problems, any measure that succeeds in reducing crime will probably have benefits that go far beyond this. Early prevention that reduces offending would probably also reduce drinking, drunk driving, drug use, sexual promiscuity and family violence, and perhaps also school failure, unemployment and marital disharmony.

It is clear from the Cambridge Study that the most persistent offenders start early, have long criminal careers, and have difficulties in many aspects of their lives. Furthermore, we know that persistent offenders tend to produce the next generation of delinquent children. It is important to target children at risk with prevention programmes in childhood in order to break this cycle of intergenerational transmission.

Publications

Up to January 2009, there have been 166 publications from the Cambridge Study. The current list of publications can be downloaded from David Farrington's page on the Institute of Criminology website.

Chapter 6

The Institute's Research Centres

The first two Research Centres within the Institute were established in 2000 – they were the Prisons Research Centre and the Centre for Penal Theory and Penal Ethics. Then from 2002 to 2007, after a successful bid for funding, the Institute was the base for a collaborative ESRC-funded Research Network on Social Contexts of Pathways in Crime (SCoPiC), led by Professor Per-Olof Wikström and involving King's College London and the Universities of Sheffield and Huddersfield as well as Cambridge. The largest empirical study within the SCoPiC Network was led by Per-Olof Wikström and was conducted in Peterborough. Funding was subsequently obtained from the ESRC for a further five years of work in Peterborough (2007–12), now conducted within the 'PADS+ Research Centre'.

The most recent Research Centre in the Institute is the Jerry Lee Centre for Experimental Criminology, generously funded by the Jerry Lee Foundation after the appointment of Professor Lawrence Sherman as the fourth Wolfson Professor in 2007.

The Prisons Research Centre

The Prisons Research Centre (PRC) was formally established in 2000, with initial funding from the Prison Service, in response to growing interest in the prisons research being conducted at the Institute of Criminology under Professor Alison Liebling. The orienting theme of the work being conducted in the Centre is 'shaping prison life', and its collective research programme aims to provide a close documentation and analysis of both the internal dynamics of prisons and the nature of penal practice in a rapidly-changing society. Within this broad framework, the Centre's more specific aims are: (i) to provide a stimulating research environment in which a coherent strategy of applied and theoretical research on prisons can be facilitated, and (ii) to develop a new generation of prisons researchers.

Since its inception, the Centre has generated funding of more than £1 million, and has seen several major research projects as well as PhD theses through to completion. The long-term and integrated nature of the work being conducted provides 'added value' to the prisons research community.

A significant number of the Centre's current research projects have developed out of research aimed at measuring 'moral climates' in prisons using carefully designed prisoner and staff surveys. This type of survey was formally adopted by the Prison Service for routine use in all prisons in 2002.

Interest in this type of measurement dwindled when faith in the potential for prisons to rehabilitate declined during the 1980s. More recently, attempts at measurement of prison regimes have returned, but they initially tended to concentrate on internal organisational performance rather than on outcomes for prisoners. Hence, some prison staff, as well as critics of prison policy, expressed considerable discomfort about what they felt was the impoverished version of prison performance imposed by some of these managerialist measurement techniques. But moving

Deborah Drake, an Institute researcher, working in Wandsworth Prison, 2006.

beyond such indicators was not straightforward, because there was considerable disagreement about what ought to be measured in prison as well as doubts about what it is possible to measure. Accordingly, a year-long research project was conducted aimed at working closely with staff and prisoners in five prisons, in order to identify what matters most in prison, and therefore what should be measured. Prisoners were clear that what made one prison different from another was the manner in which they were treated by staff, how safe the prison felt, whether or not they had access to their families, and how trust and power flowed through the institution. What prisoners would measure, if they were asked and encouraged to think about this task in creative and appreciative ways, is: respect, humanity, trust, staff-prisoner relationships, safety, order, fairness, personal development, family contact and their own subjective well-being (see generally Alison Liebling with Helen Arnold, *Prisons and their Moral Performance*, 2004).

The PRC team learned to measure these things, with the help of staff and prisoners, and the results have been illuminating and statistically predictive. Low 'moral performance' (poor relationships with staff, and low perceptions of fairness and respect) is linked to higher levels of suicide and distress, and to disorder. This research has implications for prison evaluation and for our understanding of the potential of moral reasoning exercises in offending behaviour work. The version of the PRC's moral climates questionnaire that has been adopted by the Prison Service is known as MQPL (Measuring the Quality of Prison Life).

One important recent aspect of the work of the PRC is the focus on prison officers as key agents in prison life. Several research projects have looked at

Professor Alison Liebling, Director of the Prisons Research Centre.

Alison Liebling

Alison Liebling studied Politics at York University followed by a Master's degree at the University of Hull. She worked on a Home Office study of young offender throughcare with Professor Keith Bottomley from 1986–7, before undertaking her PhD on suicides in prison, at Cambridge. She attracted research fellowships from Trinity Hall, Leverhulme and the ESRC between 1991 and 2000, enabling her to carry out research on staff-prisoner relationships, the work of prison officers, the links between vulnerability to suicide and poor coping in prison, small units for difficult prisoners, incentives and earned privileges, and prison privatisation. Her main interests lie in the role of values in criminal justice work, in the links between offending and vulnerability to suicide, the flow of trust, power and authority in prison, the role of fairness, and concepts of safety.

In 2000 she was appointed Lecturer at the Institute of Criminology and became Director of the Prisons Research Centre. In 2003 she was promoted to Reader, and in 2006 to Professor of Criminology and Criminal Justice. During this time she has carried out research on measuring the quality of prison life, or the prison's 'social and moral climate', the effectiveness of suicide prevention strategies in prison, and values, practices and outcomes in public and private sector corrections. She has published several books, including *Suicides in Prison* (1992) and *Prisons and their Moral Performance: A Study of Values, Quality and Prison Life* (2004). She has also edited (with Shadd Maruna) *The Effects of Imprisonment* (2005). She has published widely in criminological journals, and is on the editorial boards of *Punishment and Society: the International Journal of Penology*; and of the Oxford University Press *Clarendon Series in Criminology*. She has acted as an advisor to several committees and jurisdictions on prisons and prisons research.

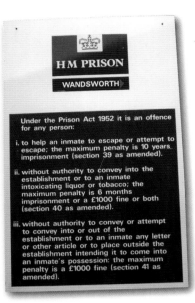

officers at their best, as well as at what happens when prison work goes wrong. The core of prison officer work is the use of discretion and authority. Together these projects have provided an important agenda for reflecting about the recruitment, training and socialisation of prison officers, mechanisms of accountability and the management of prison staff. The empirical studies on which *The Prison Officer* – Alison Liebling's co-authored ethnographic study of prison officers (Liebling and Price 2001) – is based found that the best aspects of prison officer work are their skilled peacekeeping work with prisoners and the careful use of discretion for legitimacy rather than against it. Much of this research was based on an appreciative exploration of prison officers at their best.

PhD work by Sarah Tait in the PRC has shown that prison officers have a significant impact on determining prisoner wellbeing and preventing suicide in prison. This is increasingly important as prisons accommodate more vulnerable people.

Thinking of prison work as 'care work' shapes our understanding of the ideal skills and qualities of a modern prison officer. Helen Arnold's PhD work has shown that good officers have moral strength, personal integrity, self-assuredness, empathy for the prisoner's situation and an understanding of human nature and individual needs and pains; they treat prisoners in a fair and consistent manner, are able to adapt quickly to changing circumstances, act with professionalism, and have a sense of humour. One of the key abilities common to good officers is selecting the right skill to use at the right time and to what degree, when dealing with different situations and people.

Ben Crewe's post-doctoral study of social life in an English medium-security prison found that recent years have seen concerted attempts by Prison Service senior managers to secure compliance over their institutions, their staff and the prisoners in their charge. Organisational compliance has entailed an increasingly centralised approach to prison management, in which individual establishments have considerably less autonomy to set the terms by which they operate (for example, their regime hours and practices). These efforts to reform, homogenise and closely audit how prisons function have had a significant impact on the role and power of prison officers and on the experience of prison life for prisoners. It is no longer enough for prisoners to move through a sentence passively and compliantly. Instead, they are expected to engage enthusiastically with their sentence plans and actively address their offending behaviour. Engagement with officers (and other staff) is highly advisable for anyone seeking to expedite their progression to release. Staff-prisoner relationships are therefore more 'sticky' – the outcome of mutual compulsion as much as genuine engagement. The reduction of social distance between prisoners and staff is related to the development of more humane staff cultures, but it is also an outcome of prisoners' attempts to obtain positive reports and gain minor advantages in enhancing their living standards.

The largest project currently under way in the Centre is a major study of values, practices and outcomes in public and private sector prisons. This research is funded by the ESRC over a 30-month period, and brings together the research interests of several individuals working in the Centre, in prisoner evaluations and well-being, staff deployment and culture, modern prisoner experiences, and changing management practices, together with an attempt to explore and explain different outcomes. There have been very few systematic evaluations of the effects or processes of private sector competition, so this research aims to fill that gap. The research involves interviewing and shadowing senior managers in the public and the private sector, conducting an ethnographic study of four establishments (two public and two private), conducting staff and prisoner surveys in others and watching prisons 'in transition' – that is, into a cluster, or going through a change of ownership. Emerging findings suggest that the public-private sector debate is more complex than most critics appreciate, and that each sector has significant strengths and weaknesses. Much can be learned from examining these strengths and weaknesses closely.

Current promising PhD projects under way in the Centre include an exploration of well-being and quality of life in public and private sector prisons. The National Offender Management Service (NOMS) are supporting this work with access and interest, and modest funding, although the bulk of the research grant quite properly comes from the ESRC as a neutral and independent funder. The apparently low suicide rate in private prisons seemed to indicate that prisoner well-being might be higher in some private prisons, perhaps because prisoners felt less 'deeply' imprisoned in institutions where the Prison Officers' Association does not operate (reflected in findings from our evaluation of the 'safer custody' project, and the study above). So we designed a study that would hold performance and ownership constant, in order to investigate these issues more carefully. Another current PhD research project examines what makes an effective senior management team, using extended observation and interviews with highly recommended senior managers and their staff.

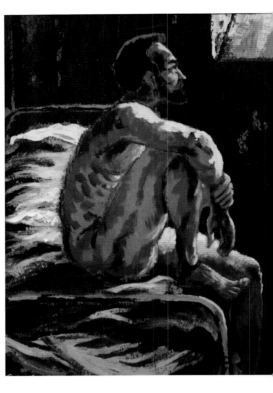

Still Life Prisoner, by Colin Lyons, an inmate of HM Prison Dartmoor. It was bought for the Library through the Koestler Trust for Arts Inside.

One of the very useful pieces of advice our Steering Group members gave us at an early meeting was to diversify the Centre's sources of research income so that Prison Service and Home Office funding did not dominate. This was quickly achieved, so that currently several of our largest projects are funded by other bodies, including the ESRC, the Leverhulme Trust, the KPMG Foundation and the Nuffield Foundation.

The Centre works closely with the Prison Service's Standards Audit Unit, advising on the development and interpretation of the MQPL survey. There have been requests to use versions of the MQPL survey in other jurisdictions, including Norway, Sweden, the USA, Australia and Israel. Professor Liebling joined the Western Australian (WA) Prisons Inspectorate on a Thematic Review of deaths in custody in 2005, as well as undertaking a review of WA's only private prison in 2007. Both of these exercises were highly informative. We have also responded to ad hoc requests from the Prison Service to host seminars on, for example, professional standards, the development of senior officers, and suicide prevention, as well as visiting prisons experiencing high numbers of suicides to conduct ad hoc MQPL surveys, and to attend and speak at national and area conferences about our work. Closer to home, much research-led teaching is conducted in the Institute by members of the Centre, and students find it attractive to carry out their research in such an active environment.

The Centre for Penal Theory and Penal Ethics

The Centre for Penal Theory and Penal Ethics was established in October 2000. Its purpose is to explore normative and ethical issues in contemporary criminal law and criminal policy. Andrew von Hirsch is the Centre's Director, Sir Anthony Bottoms is Associate Director, and Andrew Simester (now at the National University of Singapore) is Senior Research Fellow.

The idea for the Centre grew out of a colloquium on situational crime prevention ('SCP') in Cambridge which Professor von Hirsch organised in early 1997. 'Situational crime prevention' is criminologists' term for crime-prevention strategies (such as 'target hardening' or improved surveillance) aimed at reducing criminal opportunities in the routines of everyday life. While SCP had attracted much discussion, its focus was on effectiveness and technical questions – eg, does closed-circuit television surveillance 'work' in deterring offenders? More theoretical issues, especially ethical ones, had received little attention.

The 1997 colloquium brought together a group of legal philosophers and criminologists to examine these latter issues. The discussion proved most stimulating, suggesting the usefulness of examining contemporary criminological issues from a wider (particularly, normative) standpoint.

The Centre was conceived as a vehicle to facilitate inquiries of this kind. Its function would be to bring contemporary currents of thinking and policy on criminal law, punishment and crime prevention under new scrutiny, and particularly to consider their ethical and philosophical dimensions.

The Penal Theory Centre is thus a little different from the other Research Centres within the Institute. Whereas each of the other Centres is built especially around an ongoing programme of empirical research, the primarily theoretical (and especially philosophical) orientation of the Penal Theory Centre means that its work is best advanced through colloquia. Moreover, a distinctive methodology has been developed for the Centre's projects. For each project, two colloquia are held. In the first, there is a general exploration of the issues in a round-table discussion, and decisions are taken as to which issues to take forward. Papers are then commissioned, and are prepared in advance of the second colloquium, where they are discussed and criticied prior to their publication.

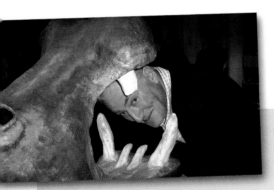

Professor Andrew von Hirsch, Director of the Centre for Penal Theory and Penal Ethics, who has a particular fondness for hippos. This one is a papier maché sculpture made by young offenders in HMYOI and RC Brinsford and bought by the Radzinowicz Library through the Koestler Trust for Arts Inside.

Andrew von Hirsch

Andrew von Hirsch was born in Switzerland of German parents, and raised in Italy, England and the US. He did his undergraduate studies in philosophy at Harvard, and has a law degree from the same university. Before coming to Cambridge, he spent two decades teaching at the Graduate School of Criminal Justice at Rutgers University. He became Honorary Professor of Penal Theory and Penal Law at Cambridge in 1996, and has been at the Institute since.

Recently, he has also been named Honorary Professor at the Law Faculty of the University of Frankfurt, Germany. He holds an honorary doctorate of law from Uppsala University, Sweden, and an LLD from Cambridge.

Von Hirsch's primary interests relate to the normative and ethical foundations of criminal law and policy. He has written extensively on the rationale of criminal sentencing – and especially on the role of sentence proportionality. His books on the topic include *Doing Justice* (1976), *Past or Future Crimes* (1985), *Censure and Sanctions* (1993), and *Proportionate Sentencing* (2005, with Andrew Ashworth). Since the 1990s, he has turned his attention also to 'criminalisation' – the scope and moral limits of criminal prohibitions. In this area, for example, he has written on legal paternalism and on prohibitions of offensive and 'antisocial' behaviour.

A decade ago, von Hirsch established and continues to direct the Centre for Penal Theory and Penal Ethics at the Institute. He also has recently established a second research centre on penal theory, at the University of Frankfurt.

To date, four major Centre projects have been completed and a fifth has reached an advanced stage. A brief sketch of each of these projects follows:

1. *Situational Crime Prevention.* As already mentioned, this was the Centre's first major effort. Some participants in the 1997 colloquium on SCP were subsequently asked to write papers, which were reviewed at a follow-up 1999 meeting (while the Centre was being organised). A number of ethical and conceptual issues were addressed: To what extent do situational crime prevention strategies (eg CCTV surveillance) interfere with citizens' freedom or entitlement to anonymity in public space? How does SCP alter criminological discourse: to what extent, for example, does it 'normalise' the treatment of crime, to become an everyday risk to be managed? Participants in the project included Ronald Clarke, Adam Crawford, Antony Duff, David Garland, Andrew von Hirsch, Tim Hope, John Kleinig, Sandra Marshall, Clifford Shearing, Joanna Shapland, David Smith, Richard Sparks, and Alison Wakefield. The product of this effort was a collection of essays that appeared in 2000, as the first volume in the Centre's series, 'Studies in Penal Theory and Penal Ethics', which is published by Hart Publishing (see von Hirsch et al. 2000).

2. *Restorative Justice.* The Centre's second major project concerned restorative justice (RJ). The restorative justice movement has recently become very influential, especially in the US and a number of Commonwealth countries. Restorative justice deals with criminal offences by involving the offender, victim, and community representatives in an informal negotiating process, usually leading to the offender's making an apology, undertaking a 'reparative' task and, sometimes, agreeing to a rehabilitative programme. There is a voluminous, but rather uncritical, literature on this subject. RJ's stated aims are frequently ambitious – that the victim be 'restored', the 'conflict' between offender and victim healed, the community be reassured, etc. The precise meanings of these varying aims as well as their interrelations have remained unclear, however – as have been the dispositional criteria that would advance these aims and the limits that should apply to restorative dispositions. Also, in practice RJ processes sometimes replace, but are sometimes added to, more traditional criminal justice procedures.

The Centre's project on RJ was entitled: 'Restorative Justice and Criminal Justice: Competing or Reconcilable Paradigms?', and it aimed to bring greater clarity to many of the theoretical issues surrounding RJ. A group of criminologists and legal philosophers from a number of countries convened in Cambridge in October 2000 and brought both supportive and critical perspectives on RJ to bear. A second follow-up colloquium took place in Toronto in April 2001. Issues addressed included specifying restorative justice's aims more clearly, examining what limiting principles (eg proportionality constraints) should apply, and examining how RJ might relate to other, more traditional penal strategies.

Participants in the centre's colloquia usually come from outside as well as within the UK, and the RJ project in particular benefitted from multi-national participation. Contributors to the final volume were: from the UK, Andrew Ashworth, Anthony Bottoms, James Dignan, Antony Duff, Andrew von Hirsch, Carolyn Hoyle, Barbara Hudson, Paul Roberts, Joanna Shapland and Richard Young; from Canada, Kent Roach and Julian Roberts; from Australasia, John Braithwaite, Kathleen Daly, Gabrielle Maxwell, Allison Morris and Clifford

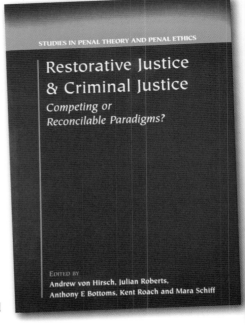

A volume in the Institute's book series on 'Studies in Penal Theory and Penal Ethics', published by Hart Publishing.

Shearing; from the United States, Leena Kurki, Mara Schiff and Daniel van Ness; and from Belgium, Lode Walgrave The resulting volume appeared as the second in the Centre's series (von Hirsch et al. 2003).

3. *The Legal Prohibition of Incivilities or 'Offensive' Behaviour.* In most jurisdictions, the criminal law has long contained a number of prohibitions against behaviour that is considered to be 'offensive', but does not cause physical or material harm (eg indecent exposure). Several jurisdictions – most ambitiously, England and Wales – are now significantly extending the reach and severity of such prohibitions. Included have been harsher measures against (even peaceable) begging, and the legal authorisation of prohibitory orders (with severe breach sanctions) against 'antisocial' conduct. Because of the scope and potential severity of such quality-of-life prohibitions, it is essential to fashion principles regarding their aims and limits.

A third research project of the Centre has explored such questions. The issues considered concern the conception of offensiveness itself (must it involve some harm? If not, should it suffice that the conduct is widely disliked, or must treating others disrespectfully be involved?). What social factors have generated the current political interest in cracking down on 'incivilities'?

A first colloquium on this topic of offensive behaviour was held in Cambridge in October 2002, with a follow-up meeting reviewing participants' drafts in the autumn of 2004. Participants included Anthony Bottoms, Elizabeth Burney, Antony Duff, Andrew von Hirsch, Tatjana Hornle, Douglas Husak, Sandra Marshall, Paul Roberts, Andrew Simester, John Tasioulas and Bryan Turner. The papers, revised and edited, appeared as the third volume in the Centre's series (see von Hirsch and Simester 2006).

4. *Strict Liability in Criminal Law.* Criminal liability without fault (that is, without need to prove the defendant's criminal intent or recklessness) has long been considered unfair by many legal commentators, yet it is used extensively in English and American law. However, the reasons for its unfairness, and the possible exceptions where it might be more defensible, have not been debated in much depth.

A Centre project has undertaken such an examination. A discussion colloquium was held in Cambridge in May 2002 with a second colloquium to review papers in the following year. Professor Simester took the lead; other participants included Andrew Ashworth, Antony Duff, John Gardner, Stuart P. Green, Jeremy Horder, Douglas Husak, Alan Michaels, Antje Pedain, Paul Roberts, John Spencer and G.R. Sullivan. The resulting papers appeared in 2005 as a volume published by Oxford University Press (Simester 2005).

5. *The Role of Previous Convictions in the Determination of Sentence.* The Centre's most recent project has focused on an important topic in criminal sentencing. After the seriousness of the crime, prior convictions are in many jurisdictions the most important factor actually relied upon to decide sentence. There is, however, extensive divergence of opinion about why and to what extent previous convictions should be deemed relevant to sentence.

Utilitarian penal theorists, such as James Q. Wilson, argue that the prior criminal record should be the primary factor in sentence, as it best predicts the offender's likelihood of recidivism. Some retributivist theorists, such as George Fletcher, advocate the contrary view: that previous

Conference of the Penal Theory Centre, 2009. Delegates included (l to r)Kevin Reitz (University of Minnesota), Martin Wasik (University of Keele), Lila Kazemian (John Jay College, New York), Michael Tonry (University of Minnesota), Peter Asp (University of Stockholm), Andrew von Hirsch, Yongjae Lee (Fordham University, New York), Anthony Bottoms, Estella Baker (University of Sheffield). Photo by Helen Jack.

offending should play no role at sentencing at all, since previous convictions do not affect the seriousness of the offender's current crime. Other retributivists, including Andrew von Hirsch and Andrew Ashworth, maintain that previous convictions should have a limited role to play at sentencing, by providing a modest initial discount, which gradually diminishes with repetitions. More recently, critiques of both these latter two positions have emerged. The debate about the role of an offender's previous convictions has thus become quite lively.

However, there has been little systematic comparison and analysis of these various perspectives. The fifth major project of the Centre has aimed to fill that void by examining in depth the theory and practice of adjusting sentences to take account of an offender's prior convictions. A first colloquium on this subject was held in Cambridge in May 2008, with a follow-up meeting in Oxford in April 2009. Participants include Andrew Ashworth, Estella Baker, Chris Bennett, Anthony Bottoms, Richard Frase, Lila Kazemian, Joungjae Lee, Kevin Reitz, Julian Roberts, Michael Tonry, Andrew von Hirsch and Martin Wasik. The resulting collection of essays will be published by Hart Publishing, Oxford, as a further volume in the Centre's series.

In addition to its main focus on specific projects, the Centre has maintained an active programme for Visiting Fellows and scholars, aimed at giving them the opportunity to conduct their own research in Cambridge, to participate in colloquia, and to develop ideas on penal theory in discussions with Centre staff.

Visiting Fellows are senior academic visitors who are given office space at the Institute for a term. They have included Douglas Husak (Rutgers, Philosophy), Andrew Simester (Nottingham, Law), Tatjana Hornle (Munich, Law), Kurt Seelmann (Basel, Law), Wolfgang Wohlers (Zurich, Law), and Ulfrid Neumann (Frankfurt/Main, Law). Visiting scholars are younger academics conducting research in the areas of the Centre's interests. These have included Josep Cid (Barcelona, Criminology), Karsten Gaede (Zurich, Law), Nina Persak (Ljubljana, Law), and Anna Leonarda Girardi (Foggia, Law).

The PADS+ Research Centre

The PADS+ Research Centre, headquarters of the Peterborough Adolescent and Young Adult Development Study (PADS+), was established, under ESRC funding, in 2002, as part of the SCoPiC Research Network (see the introduction to this chapter). Its main objective is to advance our understanding of the causes and prevention of young people's crime involvement by studying:

- the interaction between personal characteristics and experiences and the features of the social environments in which young people spend their time;
- how these interactions change over time, and how this shapes criminal involvement over two critical developmental phases: adolescence and the transition into young adulthood.

Opposite: Professor Per-Olof Wikström with Professor Dan Nagin of the Carnegie-Mellon University at the annual SCoPiC conference hosted by the Institute in 2005.

Researcher Caroline Moul interviewing a participant in the Peterborough Adolescent and Young Adult Development Study, 2008. Photo by Beth Hardie.

Professor Per-Olof H. Wikström

The hallmark of P-O Wikström's academic career has been the pursuit of his interest in bridging the gap between individual and environmental approaches to crime causation and prevention. He was born in 1955 and grew up mostly in the city of Gävle (often referred to, at the time, as the 'Chicago of Sweden' due to its high levels of violent crime). He moved to Stockholm in 1974 and completed his BA (sociology, psychology and criminology) at the University of Stockholm in a record two years, but continued his undergraduate studies for several more years (attending courses in political science, economic history and philosophy), before embarking on his PhD on 'individual, situational and ecological aspects of crimes of violence'. After completing his PhD in 1985 he was offered a job at the Research Department of the Swedish National Crime Prevention Council (Scandinavia's largest criminological research institution at the time) where he stayed for ten years, the last five as Head of the Research Department. During this period he was also appointed adjunct Professor of Sociology of Crime at the University of Stockholm. He left the Council in 1995 due to a disagreement about the future direction of the Council's research and moved to the Swedish National Police College, where he helped build its Research Unit. After a short spell at the Police College, he was invited to apply for a post at the University of Cambridge and moved to the Institute of Criminology in 1997, where he has been ever since. In 1994 he received the American Society of Criminology's Sellin-Glueck Award for outstanding international contributions to criminology and in 2002 was made a Fellow of the highly prestigious Center for Advanced Study in the Behavioral Sciences in Stanford (USA).

Explicitly, the Centre seeks to further our understanding of why young people engage in crime – ie, what causes them to become involved in, stay involved in and stop being involved in crime. To do so, the Centre is working to identify different pathways of individual development and their relationship to different patterns of crime involvement, as well as key personal and environmental factors whose interaction may lead young people to embark on specific pathways.

Such knowledge is crucial for the effective targeting of prevention efforts because it helps us to better understand what kinds of interventions are likely to be most effective for what kinds of young people in what kinds of social environments (and why). The ultimate aim of PADS+ is therefore to better inform policy and practice about the causes of young people's crime and thereby to improve prevention and intervention.

Behaviours arise from the interaction between people and their environments. Young people are particularly susceptible to external influences, especially during adolescence. As they mature, young people undergo physiological and psychological changes which generally increase their mobility and agency. This, in turn, often leads to changes in their exposure to different social environments and, consequently, their behaviour. Yet the social environment remains one of the least understood factors in young people's crime involvement. PADS+ seeks to obtain a better understanding of its role by studying the relationship between changes in young people and their exposure to different social environments and changes in their crime involvement during adolescence.

Young people differ both in their personal characteristics and life experiences and the social environments in which they live and develop. By observing young people and their environments during the critical developmental period between adolescence and young adulthood, the PADS+

Research Centre hopes to gain a better understanding of the factors which lead some young people to become involved, and stay involved, in crime.

The main activities of the PADS+ Research Centre revolve around PADS+, a major longitudinal study following a group of more than 700 young people living in Peterborough who were randomly selected from their age group in 2002, when they were 11 years old. These young people have taken part annually in one-to-one interviews and small-group questionnaires with trained researchers. Their parents also took part in the first data wave (2003), providing retrospective data.

The research team has been active in tracking participants and motivating participation. As a result the study has maintained admirable retention rates. More than 96% of the sample has taken part in each of the first six waves (2003–8). With three more years of theory-driven, longitudinal research on the horizon, PADS+ expects to provide a robust evidence base concerning young people, their social environments, and their crime involvement. This can be used to develop innovative strategies for tackling young people's offending.

PADS+ research has been designed around a robust theoretical framework – the Situational Action Theory (SAT) (Wikström 2006, 2010 [forthcoming]) – which addresses key shortcomings in criminological theory by presenting a clear definition of crime and taking into account both personal and environmental factors which play a causal role in young people's crime involvement, and their interaction. SAT explains crimes as moral actions – actions which break rules about what it is right or wrong to do in a given setting – focusing on causal factors which relate to personal moral rules and emotions (eg, shame and guilt) and moral contexts (rules which apply to a particular setting and their level of enforcement), as well as factors which influence their development and emergence.

PADS+ researchers have developed a new methodology to tackle the problem of measuring people's exposure to particular social environments. Previous criminological research has often

Litter in Peterborough.

operationalised the social environment as a person's neighbourhood, even though people spend time in social environments outside their neighbourhoods. PADS+, on the other hand, utilises a space-time budget to measure which social environments young people take part in, how much time they spend in those environments, and what they do within them. Using a detailed time diary, the space-time budget collects information about young people's activities over four days in a typical week (Friday and Saturday plus two other weekdays). This data includes:

- where they were (the geographic location – ie, the census output area)
- where they were (the behaviour setting – eg, home, school, shopping centre, park)

Peterborough city centre. Photo courtesy of Peterborough Tourist Information Centre.

- who they were with (eg, peers, parents, other adult guardians)
- what they were doing (their main activity, including crime involvement and drug use)

When aggregated, these data provide information about how much time each young person spends in certain settings (for example, away from home or school) with certain people (for example, peers and no adult guardian), and what he/she tends to do in those settings (for example, structured or unstructured activities). From this we can learn what kinds of social situations young people tend to be in when they are involved in crime.

This space-time budget data is used in conjunction with social environmental data collected via the Peterborough Community Survey (PCS), a large-scale postal survey of the PADS+ study area. This survey provides data on factors such as informal social control, social cohesion and 'collective efficacy' (residents' and others' willingness to enforce social norms) for each census output area covered. Using combined data from space-time budgets and the PCS, researchers can determine the amount of time young people spend in different kinds of social environments (their exposure to different social contexts).

PADS+ also collects data using more traditional methodologies, which when combined with space-time budget and PCS data present a complex and detailed picture of how certain kinds of young people relate to and interact with certain kinds of social environments, helping to identify situations in which this interaction can lead to offending. These methodologies include:

- young person and parent questionnaires (which gather data on young people's family life, school experiences, peer groups and neighbourhoods as well as personal characteristics like personal moral rules and emotions and generalised self-control)
- various neuropsychological measures (which gauge cognitive capabilities relevant to moral decision making, including habituation and the ability to exercise self-control)

Through this wealth of data, PADS+ researchers hope to begin answering important questions about the causes of young people's crime involvement. Key areas of interest to the study include:

- the interplay between young people's morality and self-control
- young people's differential exposure to social and moral contexts
- how family social position (class, income and education) and family and school social bonds affect the development of morality and self-control and young people's exposure to different moral contexts

- the role of social environmental factors such as informal social control, social integration, social cohesion, and collective efficacy in young people's moral development and crime involvement
- the role of broader social processes (eg residential and school segregation and neighbourhood disadvantage) and background personal factors (eg ethnicity, gender, religion, family structure and family changes) in young people's crime involvement

As the participants enter young adulthood, the study has begun collecting data on family formation, partner violence, labour market experiences, and their link to changing and continued crime involvement. The study is also beginning to collect relevant official data on its participants from a variety of sources, including schools and police data.

Early findings from PADS+ underscore the importance of the interaction between individual characteristics, especially moral rules and emotions, and environmental factors such as monitoring and supervision, as well as the importance of separating causes of crime (such as having moral rules and emotions conducive to crime) from more distant causes of the causes (such as disadvantage). As an illustration, Figure 1 (opposite) shows that from the ages of 12–16, participants with low 'crime propensity' (a combined measure of their personal morality and ability to exercise self-control) were unlikely to offend regardless of how much time they spent in criminogenic settings (ie settings in which they were unsupervised with their peers in areas with low collective efficacy), while participants with medium and high propensity offended at a higher rate if they spent more time in criminogenic settings. This relationship was particularly strong for those with high propensity. Interestingly, participants with low propensity were also unlikely to spend a significant amount of time in criminogenic settings, while participants with high propensity were unlikely not to, suggesting the relationship is more complex than the figure can capture, and may need to take into account developmental or selection effects.

Relative to other studies in criminology and related disciplines, PADS+ provides a unique perspective on

- young people in a contemporary and therefore highly relevant cohort
- their personal characteristics and life experiences, especially during the important time-window between adolescence and young adulthood
- the social environments to which they are exposed
- the degree to which they are exposed to those environments
- their crime involvement

Taken together, this knowledge can help advance our understanding of the direct causes of young people's crime, as well as the causes of the causes, providing a clearer foundation for developing prevention and intervention strategies. Because PADS+ is constructed around a strong theoretical framework which draws upon existing knowledge from multiple disciplines and utilises robust methodologies to ensure the quality and detail of its data, it has very real potential to improve our knowledge about why and how young people become involved in crime and, consequently, how to effectively intervene.

As PADS+ enters its seventh year, it is attracting collaborative interest from researchers and research centres around the world and has already begun promoting cross-comparative studies in several European countries. Although its primary research remains based in the UK,

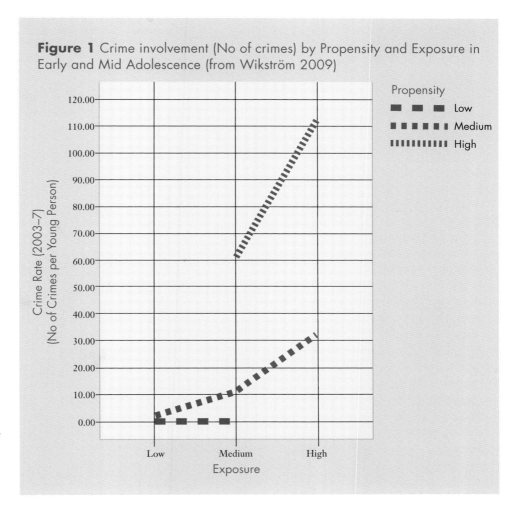

Figure 1 Crime involvement (No of crimes) by Propensity and Exposure in Early and Mid Adolescence (from Wikström 2009)

A PADS+ model showing criminality levels by 'crime propensity' and 'exposure to criminogenic settings'.

PADS+ is becoming an increasingly 'international' research centre. It has brought a number of distinguished visitors, guest speakers and postdoctoral researchers to Cambridge from abroad, and will continue to do so in the future. Its theoretical framework and robust data have international appeal and relevance, and its findings may consequently have widespread significance for the study and prevention of young people's crime.

For more about PADS+, please visit our website: www.pads.ac.uk

The Jerry Lee Centre of Experimental Criminology

The Jerry Lee Centre of Experimental Criminology is the newest of the Research Centres at the Institute of Criminology. It conducts and synthesises randomised controlled trials of policing, criminal justice and crime prevention programmes, as well as training doctoral and post-doctoral students in the methods and practices of experiments in crime and justice. The Centre's mission is to produce better evidence for advancing human liberty. Experimental criminology is a rapidly growing field, with increasing influence on public policy decisions. The Jerry Lee Foundation of Philadelphia decided in 2006 to offer to help found the world's first university centre devoted solely to the advancement of experimental criminology. It seemed appropriate to locate it at Cambridge University, since this branch of criminology uses a scientific method that was invented by a Cambridge graduate and Professor of Genetics, Sir Ronald Aylmer Fisher, whose theoretical work on experimental methods revolutionised the study of cause and effect. Among his many ideas was the central insight that random assignment of a consistent action across some but not all of a large population could 'hold constant' the other factors that could affect any subsequent outcomes.

With the Lee Foundation's initial pledge to fund a programme of pre-doctoral and post-doctoral 'Jerry Lee Scholars,' the University agreed to have the Jerry Lee Centre of Criminology established in the Institute of Criminology in 2007. In that same year Lawrence Sherman, the University's fourth Wolfson Professor of Criminology, was appointed the first Director of the Jerry Lee Centre while continuing to be Director of the Jerry Lee Center of Criminology at the University of Pennsylvania.

Experimental criminology is the use of advanced experimental methods to answer key questions about the causes and responses to crime, such as:

- How much crime does prison prevent – or cause – for different kinds of offenders?
- Does visible police patrol prevent crime everywhere or just in certain locations?
- What is the best way for societies to prevent crime from an early age?
- How can murder be prevented among high-risk groups of young men?

These and other urgent questions can be answered most clearly by the use of a research design called the 'randomised controlled trial'. This method takes large samples of people – or places, or schools, prisons, police beats or other units of analysis – who might become, or have already been, involved in crimes, either as victims or offenders. It then uses a statistical formula to select a portion of them for one treatment, and (with equal likelihood) another portion to receive a different treatment. Any difference, on average, in the two groups in their subsequent rates of crime or other dimensions of life can then be interpreted as having been caused by the randomly assigned difference in the treatment. All other differences, on average, between the two groups can usually be ruled out as potential causes of the difference in outcome. That is because with large enough samples, random assignment usually assures that there will be no other differences between the two groups except the treatment being tested.

The Cambridge Centre works closely with its counterpart at the University of Pennsylvania. In collaboration with the Australian National University, these centres also jointly operate the Jerry Lee Program of Randomised Controlled Trials in Restorative Justice, a series of 12 field experiments involving over 3,000 crime victims and offenders. This is the largest programme of

Jerry Lee (left) with Denis O'Connor, HM Chief Inspector of Constabulary (centre), and Lawrence Sherman at the International Conference on Evidence-Based Policing held in Cambridge in July 2008.

Manuel Eisner

Manuel Eisner received a Master's degree in history at the University of Zurich, having spent one year of his studies at University College, London. Soon afterwards he turned to sociology, completing his PhD and then his 'habilitation' on the causes of violent crime in late modern urban environments. From 1993 to 2001 he was assistant professor in sociology at the Federal Institute of Technology in Zurich. Before he began to consider himself a criminologist he published on a variety of subjects that reflect his interest in the interlocking dynamics of social and cultural change in modern societies. These include work on 'lonely hearts' adverts during the 20th century, the political values expressed in New Year editorials of newspapers, and the dynamics of how societies address environmental issues such as water pollution.

Manuel Eisner came to the Institute in 2000 as a lecturer. In 2002 he was promoted to a Readership, and became Deputy Director of the Institute. In 2009 he gained a Personal Professorship. His principal area of research is interpersonal violence and its explanation. His goal is to contribute to the integration of macro-level – historical and cross-national – approaches to violence and micro-level explanations that consider the impact of individual development and situational dynamics. At the applied level, his work aims at contributing to better violence prevention through experimental research. Recent publications include a contribution to a general theory of violence, a study of 19th and 20th century trends in homicide across Europe, an analysis of conflict of interest as a possible confound in experimental studies, and methodological work on measuring life-events in longitudinal studies.

He is regularly involved in providing expert advice and disseminating findings on effective violence prevention to local, national and international agencies including, the Federal Government of Switzerland, the Council of Europe, the International Federation of Educative Communities (FICE) and the World Health Organisation. He is a Fellow of the Academy of Experimental Criminology.

participants are exposed to a staged crime and later interviewed about it. One study examines the effect of time of day of the interview on the accuracy of the witness. Findings show that older adults remember up to ten more accurate details, if an eyewitness interview occurs in the morning rather than in the afternoon, while young adults show no such difference. Also, by activating positive beliefs about the effect of aging on memory it is possible to increase the number of accurate details remembered, and to decrease suggestibility. These findings can be directly translated into forensic interviewing practice, eg by taking into account time of day when scheduling interviews with older witnesses, and by giving interviewers further training to set their older witnesses more at ease during the interview.

In a series of influential empirical and theoretical projects Dr Loraine Gelsthorpe explores issues relating to 'fairness', 'discretion' and 'discrimination' in the criminal justice system (Gelsthorpe and Padfield 2003). Her research has a particular focus on how far men and women are 'equal before the law' and how far 'equal treatment' should be the same treatment, given identification of both similarities and differences in terms of social background, personal problems, and criminogenic needs. Most recently, this work has included analysis of sentencing statistics relating to men and women and in relation to explanations for the increase in the 'punitive turn' towards women from the mid-1990s to 2005: recognition of 'equality in social life' and therefore 'equal sentencing', more women offenders committing more serious crimes or prisons being used as social services are key questions. 'Diversity' issues within a range of criminal justice system policies and practices have also been subject to critical scrutiny. A

Loraine Gelsthorpe

Loraine Gelsthorpe initially studied at the British School of Violin-Making, and then embarked on training as a psychiatric nurse with a view to doing music therapy. Her undergraduate course at Sussex University, her work with troubled and troublesome children and as a research assistant on a penal history project, however, inspired her to come to Cambridge to pursue the MPhil in Criminology, followed by a PhD. After research work at Lancaster University, UCNW, Bangor, and the LSE, Loraine returned to the Institute as Senior Research Associate in 1992. A University Lectureship and Senior Lectureship followed and she was awarded a Readership in 2005. Loraine was awarded a Pilkington Teaching Prize for her innovations in graduate training in 1997. She is Director of the MPhil programmes.

Broad interests include the link between criminal and social justice, developments in penal policy since 1945, discretion and discrimination. Within these fields, she has carried out innovative research on women, crime and criminal justice (see page 94) and has published extensively on issues relating to youth justice. She is also well-known for her work on community penalties with the publication of a series of cutting-edge essays in *The Handbook of Probation* (with Rod Morgan) in 2007.

Loraine is Chair of the Cambridge Socio-legal Group (a multi-disciplinary network of academics). She has served on the ESRC's Training Board and on the 2008 RAE sub-panel (Social Policy, Social Administration & Social Work), as well as acting as advisor to the Home Office on issues relating to PSRs and women and criminal justice in particular. She sits on the Editorial Boards of the *British Journal of Criminology*, *Youth Justice*, *Criminology and Criminal Justice*, *The Howard Journal* and *The Australian and New Zealand Journal of Criminology*. Loraine chairs the British Society of Criminology's Ethics Committee. She is a Fellow of the Royal Society of Arts for her contributions to criminal justice.

Loraine Gelsthorpe with MPhil student Fafunso Olawale at his graduation, 1995.

survey of provision for women offenders in the community, involving visits to a sample of sites (including both statutory and voluntary sector service providers) and interviews with key staff has proved influential. The identification of nine key precepts for good practice in terms of the treatment of women offenders within community provision, and the setting out of nine questions for commissioners of services through the work has played a role in the development of the national framework for the delivery of effective services to women offenders.

In a pioneering study involving nearly 400 lay magistrates and district judges from over 150 magistrates' courts, Dr Mandeep Dhami used an experimental approach to examine how bail decisions are made (Dhami 2001). Ideally, decision-makers ought to consistently weigh and integrate legally relevant information in a case. However, findings suggest that this ideal is far from the reality, and may be unattainable. Rather, decision-makers were inconsistent as they made different decisions on the same case presented on another occasion. They also disagreed with one another about the decision to be made on a case. Bail hearings in the courtroom were rapid. Indeed, when deciding on simulated or real cases, decision-makers used 'fast and frugal' strategies that ignored much of the relevant, available information, and sometimes relied on extra-legal information. Decision-makers, however, reported using only legally relevant information, and they were highly confident in their decisions. Given that bail decisions have ramifications for defendants and society, and may influence later decisions in a case, Dr Dhami concludes that it is necessary to determine how performance can be improved, so that due process is observed and justice is served.

Graffiti on the door of 7 West Road, 1979.

When I say that I loved the Institute from the moment I arrived, I mean that I loved all aspects of it, from the shabby shared graduate room in the back corridor of the main floor with its permeable windows, to the discussions at morning coffee and the tea break in the afternoon. The opportunity which the Institute offered for several years of wonderful interdisciplinary study on subjects which I truly think are worth spending time pursuing, was a marvel…

In the spring of 1979 I made a trip with an international Applied Economics group to Northern Ireland to visit the then most economically deprived region of Europe. What I saw captured my interest completely. I met several barristers practising before the Diplock Courts, several academic lawyers and physicians, several political leaders and stayed in a hotel which had been blown up 29 times. I was thoroughly shocked to realise that extraordinary courts could be put in place under British Common Law, something which I could never have imagined from my criminology studies in colonial, stable Canada. I realised that studying the criminalisation of politically motivated crime, and the politicisation of criminal activity was a subject which could easily compel my interest for the necessary five years it might take to complete.

Back at the Institute, someone had written 'IRA' in white spray-painted graffiti across the Institute front door, which was indeed very badly received by the Institute. Having their Danish-Canadian research student return from her travels to say that she proposed to abandon the study of Law Reform Commissions in favour of understanding how the concept of 'terrorist' and 'terrorism' could be constructed within constitutional democracies, Canada and Northern Ireland, was viewed with some trepidation by some at the Institute… Professor Walker, however, listened with great interest, asked who I had read and who I had met, and who I intended to speak to, asked if I could produce a PhD outline and a first chapter, and then called upon Professor Paul O'Higgins at Christ's ('a civil rights man') to ask if he would supervise my thesis. And as a result, I spent a happy five years delving into a subject which I loved, with Paul O'Higgins, another man of great civility, learning, and commitment, and Dr Tom Hadden, Institute graduate, writer, and lecturer at Queen's University Belfast, and happily completed my work at the Cambridge Institute in collaboration with the Law Faculty. The Institute turned out to truly have a wide wing span, held particularly wide and firm by Professor Walker's appreciation of the importance of academic freedom and respect for the pursuit of challenging subjects.

BIRTHE JORGENSEN, DIRECTOR, MEDICAL ADVISORY SECRETARIAT,
ONTARIO MINISTRY OF HEALTH AND LONG-TERM CARE (PhD 1984)

A mixed penology and police discussion group in the basement led by Dr Tim Coupe (second from right). Students were Jonathan Tottman, Stephen Ratcliffe, Dave Nicholson and Samantha Ingram.

How is punishment executed?

Sir Leon Radzinowicz's lifelong academic interest in the penal system and its contradictions is echoed in several ongoing studies on prisons and probation.

Dr Adrian Grounds's work on the psychological effects of wrongful conviction and imprisonment has been described in chapter 4. From a different perspective, Professor Roy King has examined the causes and effects of the rise of so-called 'super-maximum security custody' (or 'supermax') for prisoners deemed to be the 'worst of the worst' (King 1999). He examines why this American invention, which visited the conditions of Guantanamo Bay on US criminals long before 9/11, and which is supported by remarkably little evidence either as to why it is needed or as to its effectiveness, has become such an attractive panacea for countries from South America to the territories of the former Soviet Union. In the latest stage of his research on supermax, Roy King in 2009 revisited Oak Park Heights Prison, Minnesota, and will draw upon research on death row in Oklahoma and Utah. The key question to be asked is how prisoners serving extremely long sentences, including life without parole, survive conditions of separation bordering on perpetual solitary confinement and sensory deprivation?

Loraine Gelsthorpe (with Gilly Sharpe and Jenny Roberts) has embarked on an innovative piece of action research to evaluate an initiative by Commonweal Housing, Housing For Women, and Women in Prison. This 'Re-Unite' project involves the provision of family housing for women leaving prison so that they can quickly be reunited with their children and therefore reduce the deleterious effects of imprisonment on the women and their children alike. With housing and individual support from Women in Prison project workers the women are also helped in attempts to retrain and enter employment. The researchers are following up the women as they are released and housed, looking at indicators of resettlement for both themselves and their children. This study involves a series of interviews with the women offenders, the project workers, probation officers, teachers, employers, and other service providers who come into contact with the women and their children, as well as analysis of other 'hard' indicators of progress. The early signs are that this might serve as a useful demonstration project to encourage other housing providers.

How can Crime be Prevented?

Over the past 20 years the Institute of Criminology has also established itself firmly as a centre for research on the control and prevention of crime with world-renowned contributions by a large number of Institute staff, including Professors David Farrington, Friedrich Lösel, and Lawrence Sherman.

More particularly, David Farrington and Lawrence Sherman have played a leading role in establishing and promoting the Crime and Justice Group of the Campbell Collaboration, a worldwide research network that supports systematic reviews of evidence-based prevention and intervention in various fields. By soliciting systematic reviews on a broad range of criminal justice interventions the activities of the group have transformed the way that researchers and practitioners think about prevention and intervention in criminology. Also, Friedrich Lösel has conducted several highly influential comprehensive systematic reviews of the empirical evidence on various types of crime prevention. One study examined the evidence of over 80 studies on the effectiveness of social skills training with children and adolescents in reducing antisocial behaviour (Lösel and Beelmann 2003). The study found that social skills training is an effective approach to reducing early antisocial behaviour, although findings are stronger for short-term

In 1987, Fiji had its first military coup d'état. I was then a prosecutor at the Office of the Director of Public Prosecutions in Fiji and had been offered a Foreign and Commonwealth Office award to study for the MPhil at the Institute of Criminology in Cambridge. However, the new military government had stopped all foreign travel by Fiji citizens. I did finally manage to leave the country but arrived in Cambridge a shattered wreck. By September 1987, all the judges of the High Court of Fiji, and of the Court of Appeal had resigned and I wasn't at all sure that after I completed the year at the Institute, there would be a criminal justice system in Fiji worth being a part of.

My first impression of the Institute was that of calm. Here I was, emerging from political and legal turmoil, to be a part of an Institute which valued research, knowledge and a rational approach to criminal justice reform. The Institute gave me back my faith in the justice system. The Director was then Professor Bottoms and our tutors included Dr David Thomas and Dr Allison Morris. Not only was I able to recover my intellectual equilibrium, I was also able to write my dissertation (under the supervision of Colin Sumner) on traditional (customary) legal systems in the context of post-colonial power structures in Fiji.

My time at the Institute was a revelation in other ways. As a prosecutor, the course encouraged me to look at the justice system in a more inclusive way, and to understand penal reform with a critical perspective. Most of all, the course helped me to understand how susceptible the criminal justice system is to political manipulation. I am a judge now in the criminal jurisdiction of the High Court of Fiji and I will never forget what I learnt in that one year at the Institute.

HONOURABLE JUSTICE NAZHAT SHAMEEM, HIGH COURT OF FIJI (MPHIL 1988)

effects and smaller studies with a high control over the delivery of the programmes. In another comprehensive meta-analysis Lösel examined the evidence on various types of treatment programmes for sexual offenders. Despite a considerable heterogeneity in the reported outcomes, the meta-analysis found robust evidence for positive effects of cognitive-behavioural programmes (Lösel and Schmucker 2005).

Also, the Institute's continued interest in effective policing and situational prevention is reflected in the research conducted by Dr Tim Coupe and Dr Kate Painter. Thus, a major study by Tim Coupe examines how useful police patrols are for detecting burglary. It draws on over 3,000 cases of residential and commercial burglary incidents, comprising detailed data on different investigative stages, victims and crime scenes, and police response logs (Coupe and Blake 2006). The study conclusively demonstrates how the number of patrols deployed and patrol crewing, together with target circumstances, influence the chances of arrests. Also, the residential environment influences when and where burglaries occur and the risks of different types of offenders being seen and arrested at different sorts of target. Hence, directed patrol can be selectively deployed during daylight on weekdays in up-market areas where younger burglar groups and older burglars travelling farther by car are at work, and in darkness in poorer areas and at weekends when older, lone offenders commit burglary. At commercial premises, the chances of arrest are better when covert rather than visible CCTV, and delayed audible compared with immediately audible alarms are installed, and when premises generating the most false alarms are accorded a low priority.

In collaborative work, Kate Painter has conducted a number of evaluations on the effects of better street lighting and the use of CCTV-cameras as an approach to improving situational crime prevention. This body of work suggests that better lighting in public places can have a positive effect sometimes even in daylight hours – an interesting example of a so-called 'diffusion of benefit' sometimes found in crime prevention schemes (Painter and Tilley 1999).

One important development in this field, increasingly taken on board by governments in the UK and internationally, is the recognition that significant prevention efforts should be devoted to measures for young children and their families. This argument, with supporting evidence, is set out in *Saving Children from a Life of Crime* (Farrington and Welsh 2007). However, while much is known about measures that achieve short-term effects in small studies, there is still significant uncertainty on how effects can be maintained until adolescence and whether they can be replicated in large-scale field trials. Two ongoing large-scale studies at the Institute examine long-term effects of early intervention. A longitudinal study by Friedrich Lösel examines the effectiveness of a combined parent training and social skills intervention in a community sample of 675 children. It found that the combined programme had significant short-term effects, some of which could be maintained over four years. Similarly, the Zurich Project on the Social Development of Children randomly implemented a parenting skills programme and a school-based social skills programme, both interventions aiming to reduce externalising problem behaviours during childhood. After three years, the study has found significant positive effects of the school-based skills training on aggressive and non-aggressive child behaviours. Effects of the parent training, in contrast, were limited to change in parenting behaviour. Interestingly, the behavioural change was not visible immediately after the intervention, but could only be observed in wave four, when teachers assessed the children who had not participated in delivering the programme. This may reflect a genuine sleeper effect, ie a delayed manifestation of behaviour change after an intervention, which has also been found in several other studies.

PhD students working in the Institute, 2009.

Chapter 8

Fulfilling Wolfson's wishes: the Radzinowicz Library

The establishment of a first-class library was one of the main wishes of the Wolfson Foundation when it endowed the new Institute of Criminology (see chapter 1), At the first meeting of the then Advisory Council of the Institute, Baroness Wootton reinforced this message, and expressed the hope that 'the library would be made available to scholars from all over the world' (Radzinowicz 1988, p.104).

Professor Donald West writes:

From its earliest days, when the Library was run by Joanna Dannatt as a sideline to her duties as Institute Secretary, it has always been for me, and I suspect for many others, the heart of the Institute. Its expansion by steps, from Scroope Terrace, to West Road, to West Road extension, and finally to its present imposing accommodation, has signalled a steady improvement in size and facilities. Successive librarians, notwithstanding their differing interests, skills and styles of management, always supported by dedicated assistants, have succeeded in maintaining an atmosphere of easy-going, friendly efficiency that has earned the gratitude of generations of users.

The holdings include an impressive accumulation of official reports and inquiries as well as much else of historic and specialised interest not frequently consulted, but it has nothing of the feel of a 'museum collection'. It is above all user-friendly, catering both to the everyday work of students needing material relating to their teaching courses and to the more recondite needs of researchers probing into uncommon or abstruse topics. The literature review and background research in many successful PhD theses owe much to the library staff who have been prepared to spend time, beyond their official duties, helping students to find and access relevant references.

One needs only to look through the regularly compiled lists of accessions to see the wide variety of materials of concern to criminologists. A recent issue is divided into over 50 topics ranging from criminal psychology to housing, from child welfare to drugs, from sex crime to racism, from biography to gender studies etc. Nowhere else is one likely to find such a diverse body of relevant information drawn from such contrasting disciplines as law, medicine and economics. The only major concern scarcely represented (and this dates from a policy decision taken at the outset) is forensic science. For DNA, blood stains, post-mortem examinations and bullet wounds – the stuff of TV crime – one needs to go elsewhere.

The life of the library has coincided with the IT revolution. It is hard for the modern student to realise how relatively recent and swift has been the change. I have watched card indexes replaced by computer terminals. Many technical publications can now be accessed and downloaded from the internet and search engines can aid swift access to vast sources of specialised references. The Library has kept up with these developments and can help users take proper advantage of the opportunities now available.

Transcending all its material and technical features, the Library presents the human face of the Institute. It is where everyone comes for information. Students are in and out. Academics,

The new Radzinowicz Library.

immersed in their disparate projects, are not always around, but the Library staff are a constant and welcoming presence. Conversation is not a feature of library study, but by some mysterious tradition a visit there, where the staff know more than most where people are and what they are doing, is surprisingly helpful.

Martin Wright who was the librarian between 1964 and 1971 remembers:

The Institute's library was fortunate both in the substantial initial funding which Professor Radzinowicz was able to secure from the Ford Foundation, and in Joan Friedman who was its first qualified librarian. She built up an impressive core collection in a very short space of time, including large numbers of print-outs of microfilm, required by Radzinowicz for his great historical works. The library's other great personality in the early days was Isobel Gawler, who could be very firm but also very helpful. Although around retiring age (we never quite knew), she was only known to take one day off sick – after dislocating her shoulder in the gym!

The collection had to balance the needs of research and teaching, and already reflected the multi-disciplinary nature of criminology, with sections on penology, psychology (but mostly the psychology of offending, not the psychology of punishment!), sociology and more. Later, aspects such as victimology began to appear. We were also able to obtain some valuable historical works, such as the 1792 edition of John Howard's *State of the Prisons*. Because of Radzinowicz's multilingual background, these also included many foreign works, especially in French, German and Italian.

Joan Friedman also undertook the major work of cataloguing the collection, and classifying it using the Bliss classification, so much more elegant than the cumbersome Library of Congress scheme which was being developed at about the same time.

Students in the Library at 7 West Road.

Your Library is akin to the great mediaeval libraries that guarded knowledge, gave sanctuary and enabled great adventures even when chaos reigned in the outside world. Neatly catalogued book repositories are a different thing altogether. The Institute likes to keep close to what is happening in the front line of the legal system. To that end it lures into its orbit people like me, who are graduates but now unfamiliar with academe and not too sure about it anyway. We bring our battle-weary selves and tangled mass of undigested, mud-spattered professional experiences to try to make sense of them in ways that might be helpful.

To us, its library is the very core of the Institute of Criminology: a thoroughly modern take on the great tradition of scholarly communities. It is a multi-dimensional resource that provides not only carefully selected texts to meet almost every academic need but also what is needed for education in its widest sense; a place of safety, informed guidance, support, encouragement and unpretentious welcome.

Fortunately, fears that the transfer to the new building would sanitise out the unquantifiable aspects have been groundless. All of value blossoms there. But it spoils one so. I have not subsequently renewed my membership of an august library elsewhere. Ordering books on-line in advance, to be delivered to your desk by a silent Ms Snippy, now seems a disappointingly thin experience on which to base a robust venture – and no fun at all.

ANN CORSELLIS (CROPWOOD FELLOW)

Letter from John George Haigh, the 'acid bath' murderer (shown above in police custody), to his parents, whilst awaiting execution in 1949. He was moved from Lewes Prison to Wandsworth where he was hanged in August 1949.

The OED defines a library as 'a room or building containing a collection of books'. Unsurprisingly, this Oxonian concoction that leaves people out does not fit the library of the Cambridge Institute of Criminology. Its impenetrable system of call numbers for the books it treasures would have baffled even the great British cryptologists who broke the encoded messages sent through the German Enigma machine during World War II. The Institute's library is a warm place where books and readers can only be connected through the ministry of people: the welcoming, gentle, patient and immensely resourceful librarians minding the store. They unlock secret cupboards and open doors to secluded rooms you never knew existed. I have spent some of the happiest moments of my academic life seeking their help and leafing through the books they unmistakably located for me. I thank them deeply and hope that they will never be digitalised.

PROFESSOR JEAN-PAUL BRODEUR, INTERNATIONAL CENTRE FOR COMPARATIVE CRIMINOLOGY
UNIVERSITÉ DE MONTRÉAL (VISITING FELLOW)

The Library Today

The Library started at the original premises in Scroope Terrace with approximately 100 books. By 1962 in supposedly temporary new premises at 7 West Road, it had amazingly acquired 4,000 volumes and by 1975 the Library had 17,500 books, 8,000 pamphlets and took 200 periodical titles. Lack of space in the Victorian building meant that conditions were always fairly cramped even after the addition of an extension. Sir Leon would, we are sure, be delighted to see the Library as it is now, in the new building on the Sidgwick Site, a light airy space with plenty of

Librarian Mary Gower (facing front) on a Library punt outing to bid farewell to her predecessor Helen Krarup, who left in 2005. Behind her (l to r) are Stuart Stone, Pam Paige, Justina Molloy and Caroline Dethridge.

room to house more than 60,000 books and over 400 periodical titles and to allow users to study in comfort. Moving to the new building has also allowed the books and journals to be arranged in a much more coherent way.

Keeping the Library up-to-date has been a primary objective of successive librarians. From the start, Sir Leon Radzinowicz was assiduous in acquiring much 19th and 20th century material as well as developing a broad-based collection. From its inception it served a wide range of users, gathering more as the subject itself expanded and developed over the years. Postgraduates, undergraduates, academics, researchers, Cropwood Fellows, practitioners within criminal justice and visiting scholars and Fellows have come through the door of what is generally regarded as one of the world's greatest collections of works in criminal justice. As the world of criminology and criminal justice has grown and developed, its staff, too, have developed links with their fellow librarians both within the UK and internationally through the World Criminal Justice Library Network, of which the Radzinowicz Library was a founder member. The biennial conferences of the Network offer librarians across the world an opportunity to keep up to date with developments in one another's countries.

A large number of journals and some books are now available online, but the physical collection will always be an important part of the Library. To facilitate efficient borrowing, we now have an up-to-date self-issue system that also has the effect of allowing staff to spend longer helping readers and developing the collection. Special collections are housed in one secure room, the 'Wakefield Room', bringing Sir Leon Radzinowicz's own donated book collection (left to the Institute on his death) together with our own old and rare books.

Over the years the Library has benefited from financial gifts and from donations of publications from individuals, which are always received with great pleasure. Minutes of the Committee of Management in 1962, for example, reveal gifts of books from His Excellency

Trips to the library took on something of the experience of visiting Aladdin's cave; from the convenience of having immediate access to books, articles and reports that simply wouldn't be available at other libraries (and thereby avoiding the interminable wait associated with inter-library loans); never knowing which internationally-renowned criminologist, whether from the Institute staff or arrived from afar, one might stumble across amongst the book-stacks; the unusual experience of watching a muntjac wander past the window as one read; to hearing about the current activities of Institute alumni from the librarians who seemed to maintain an encyclopaedic awareness of such matters. In addition, I encountered a number of my closest friends for the first time in the Radzinowicz, so I have every reason to be grateful to it.

But of course the Radzinowicz has altered substantially in recent years. The transition from the cramped conditions, out-dated terminal and a card-catalogue, not to mention the solitary photocopier in the lobby of the old West Road building, to the state-of-the-art facilities offered in the library's lavish and spacious new home means that the Radzinowicz of today is unrecognisable from that of only a few years ago.

Some things have not changed though; staff and students alike will continue to benefit from the friendly and helpful service offered by the devoted library staff. My own research was aided by pointers to recently arrived books and newly published articles and I am sure many others will have benefited similarly.

DAVID BUTTERWORTH (PhD 2003)

the German Ambassador and from Professor B. Nikiforov of the USSR. Professor Manuel López Rey donated a large collection of material on criminology and human rights in 1981. The library staff have also been touched to receive donations in memory of past students who enjoyed their time here. More recently the library has been the fortunate recipient of the letters of John George Haigh who was hanged in 1949 for the murder of six people and known as the 'acid bath murderer' because of the method he used to dispose of the bodies. Vivian Robinson QC, who was subsequently elected Treasurer of the Inner Temple for 2009, an alumnus of Sidney Sussex College, gave us the letters which are important because of the insight they provide into the complexity of the criminal mind.

In 1990 Mrs Priscilla Mitchell (née Wakefield), a personal friend of Sir Leon's and one of the Institute's main benefactors (see chapter 12) gave the Institute a generous capital sum known as the Wakefield Book Fund. The income generated by this Fund has allowed the library to maintain and expand the comprehensiveness of its collections at a time when funds from other sources were (and are) becoming more and more restricted. Books purchased from the Wakefield Fund can be identified by a specially designed book plate, and today's library user will quickly appreciate just how valuable Mrs Mitchell's generosity has been and continues to be to the Radzinowicz Library.

Bust of Mrs Priscilla Mitchell (née Wakefield, 1907–2007) by Tatiana Orloff in the Radzinowicz Library.

The Library Art Collection

'What artists and offenders have in common,' said Grayson Perry in September 2007, 'is poor impulse control.'

When a man in a silk frock makes a remark like that, it's tempting to regard it as something more than anecdotal, especially when that man has won the Turner Prize.

Perry drew this parallel during his opening speech for that year's Koestler Exhibition. The exhibition is organised annually by the Koestler Trust, a charity that promotes creativity in prisons and other places of confinement. The charity's Awards Scheme, which forms the basis of the exhibition, is a national competition with categories covering visual arts, crafts, music, and creative writing; anthologies of poetry and prose are published every year. Of the prisoners and patients who enter a piece of work into the competition, around one in four wins a cash prize.

In the Radzinowicz Library, the delinquency of our own readers contributes to the cause. Each year, we spend part of the money we raise from library fines on artworks from the Koestler Exhibition. A reader returning books late may grumble at having to pay a fine but they're usually pleased when we point to a striking mosaic or sculpture and say, 'That's where your money goes'. It's more pleasing that it helps a prisoner to discover a talent that could lead to a second chance.

Geography Mythology, *2004, by an inmate of HM Prison Gartree. It was acquired for the Library through the Koestler Trust for Arts Inside.*

Chapter 9

Pathways from Cambridge: Notable Alumni

Selecting a few alumni for mention in this brief chapter inevitably carries risks: any such list is bound to have omissions, for a variety of reasons including lack of information, lack of space, selective memory and the need to give a balanced picture. What follows is therefore certainly not comprehensive: it merely gives an indication of some notable careers, mostly in the fields of criminology and criminal justice, to which the Institute is proud to have contributed. For convenience, we have divided the chapter into sections based on the Cambridge qualification obtained.

PhD Students

In his account of the early years of the Institute, Leon Radzinowicz (1988, ch 21) included a chapter on doctoral students, entitled 'The First Ones Who Aimed High'. That chapter shows that in these initial 14 years (1960–73) the Institute admitted on average one doctoral candidate a year – and all 14 were male. By contrast, nowadays the annual PhD student intake is much larger (ten in 2008), and there are usually more women than men.

The honour of being the Institute's first successful doctoral candidate belongs to Roger Hood. After a brief postdoctoral period at Durham University, Hood returned to Cambridge as an Assistant Director of Research and Secretary of the Institute from 1967 to 1973. He then moved to Oxford to fill the Readership in Criminology made vacant by Nigel Walker's appointment to the Wolfson Chair, and he remained there until his retirement in 2003 – by which time he had become a Professor, been elected as a Fellow of the British Academy, and appointed CBE. Prominent among his many research interests is the history of criminal justice, reflected in his co-authorship with Leon Radzinowicz of the fifth volume of the latter's *History of English Criminal Law and its Administration* (1986). Other very significant research contributions have been mainly in the fields of sentencing (including his magisterial *Race and Sentencing*, 1992), parole, and comparative issues relating to the use of the death penalty.

Like Roger Hood, most of the Institute's other early doctoral students became academics, spreading the message of the importance of rigorous criminological scholarship. In Britain, for example, Keith Bottomley went to Hull University as an Assistant Lecturer in 1967 to initiate the study of criminology there, and he served in the same university with distinction until his retirement as a professor in 2005, contributing to research especially in the field of prison studies. Keith Hawkins, after completing a doctorate on parole policy, became fascinated by the general field of regulation and discretion, which he pursued at the Oxford Centre for Socio-Legal Studies until his retirement as a Professor in 2006. His *Law as Last Resort: Prosecution Decision-Making in a Regulatory Agency* won the Herbert Jacob Prize of the American Law and Society Association in 2003.

Other alumni spread the Cambridge influence internationally. Duncan Chappell, for example, became a professor at Simon Fraser University, Vancouver, before returning to his native Australia to become Director of the Australian Institute of Criminology in Canberra, and

Opposite: 'The Granta' across the millpond, a firm favourite with generations of criminology students.

Below: Roger Hood, the Institute's first PhD student, now Emeritus Professor of Criminology at Oxford University.

subsequently a judge. Two others became leading Canadian criminologists. One was British-born Irvin Waller, who became a professor at the University of Ottawa, and internationally well-known as an enthusiastic policy activist, arguing vigorously in various political contexts for better services for victims, and better crime prevention strategies. The other was Richard Ericson (Universities of Toronto and British Columbia), who became a Fellow of the Royal Society of Canada and whose prolific research output has included important work on the police; the courts; the treatment of crime in the mass media; and criminal policy in the 'risk society', including the role of insurance. Sadly, Richard Ericson died in tragic circumstances in 2007.

In the post-Radzinowicz era, the Institute continued to produce strong doctoral candidates, whose careers often had a significant international dimension. For example, David Nelken, after teaching at Edinburgh and University College, London, became a professor at the University of Macerata, Italy; there he has done distinguished work in the fields of white-collar crime and comparative criminology, and in 2009 he received the Sellin-Glueck Award of the American Society of Criminology. Warren Young is a New Zealander who wrote a Cambridge thesis on the then new topic of community service orders before returning home to the Victoria University of Wellington, becoming in time both Director of its Institute of Criminology, and Professor of Law. More recently, he has moved into the policy field, where his roles have included being Deputy Secretary for Justice, and then a Law Commissioner, becoming Deputy President of the Law Commission from 2005. Andreas Kapardis, a Cypriot psychologist, also has strong legal interests: he specialises in the interaction between law and psychology, and after a number of post-doctoral years in Australia, he has returned to Cyprus, where he is heading up the creation of a new Law School in Nicosia (as well as practising his considerable skills in karate!).

Warren Young, Deputy President of the New Zealand Law Commission.

Two sociological doctorates followed. American Richard Wright returned to the US, where he has specialised in ethnographic studies of offenders in St Louis, Missouri – his books have arresting titles like *Burglars on the Job* and *Armed Robbers in Action* (Wright and Decker 1994, 1997)! He is also the current editor of the *British Journal of Sociology*. Loraine Gelsthorpe's doctorate was a nuanced study of *Sexism and the Female Offender* in the justice system (Gelsthorpe 1989). In due course she returned to the staff of the Institute, where she has devoted countless hours to helping students, as well as pursuing her own research career as one of Britain's most distinguished writers on gender and crime and on non-custodial penalties.

In the second half of the Institute's history, PhD students have been much more numerous, but of course this group is, for the most part, still at the mid-career stage, or earlier, so it is more difficult to see the overall shape of their careers. However, some force themselves on our attention. After his doctorate, Richard Sparks (no relation to his namesake, an early member of the Institute's staff), stayed at the Institute to do post-doctoral work with Tony Bottoms on social order in prisons. He later moved to the University of Keele, where he was rapidly promoted to a professorship; he then migrated to Scotland where he holds a chair at the University of Edinburgh, and is Co-Director of the Scottish Centre for Crime and Justice Research. Also now in Scotland is Mike Nellis, who worked as a social worker before doing his doctorate, and is now Professor of Social Work at Strathclyde University, after contributing powerfully to debates about the direction of the probation service in England, and researching the important topic of the electronic monitoring of offenders. Also, there is Alison Liebling, who came to the Institute for doctoral studies from Hull, where she had studied under and worked with Keith Bottomley. Her doctorate on attempted suicides in young offender institutions paved the way for a specialist career in prison studies at the Institute, where she now heads the Prisons Research Centre (see Chapter 6).

Diploma and MPhil Students

Doctoral students have of course always been outnumbered by students taking the Postgraduate Diploma in Criminology, and its successor, the MPhil. In the space available, we can only mention a few of the many who have benefited from this course in the last half-century.

The first Diploma course is a good place to start. As well as Tony Bottoms, the graduates of this course included Andrew Rutherford, who after a significant period working in the Prison Service eventually became a professor at Southampton University, specialising in writing about various reform movements in criminal justice. Another successful alumna was the Venezuelan Rosa del Olmo, who, before her death from cancer in 2001, was one of the foremost criminologists in Latin America. Her work formed a vital bridge between South American and international criminology, and interestingly she was able to combine strong interests in 'critical criminology' with significant service for the Venezuelan government. A more practical career path was chosen by another student on the first course, Tim Cook, who worked in various posts in, for example, prison welfare and services for alcoholics before eventually becoming the Clerk (Executive Director) of the significant London-based charity, the City Parochial Foundation, whose primary aim is to 'enable the poor of London to tackle poverty and its root causes'.

Two leading students on the second Diploma Course were Roy King and Sydney Norris. Roy King chose the path of academia and became a specialist in prisons research and professor at the University of Wales, Bangor. After his 'retirement' he returned to the Institute to make an invaluable contribution as Director of the MSt Penology Course. Sydney Norris joined the Civil Service and was assigned to the Home Office, where he acted as Secretary to the Advisory Council on the Penal System in its heyday in the late 1970s. His final post was as Home Office Director of Finance, but before that he had been a senior official in the Prison Department, and at one stage acted as Chairman of the Research and Advisory Group on the Long-Term Prison System, one of whose academic members was Professor Roy King!

Another alumnus who rose high in the Home Office is Paul Wiles. He studied for the Diploma in 1967–8, and later returned to join the research staff of the Institute for a brief period before moving to the University of Sheffield. He remained there for 25 years, becoming a professor, before moving to the Home Office in 1999 as Chief Scientific Advisor and Director of Research, Development and Statistics. While retaining this post, he was later also appointed as the Government Chief Social Scientist, working across several Whitehall departments. He was awarded the CB in 2005, and is also a Visiting Professor at Oxford.

Co-students with Paul Wiles on the 1967–8 course were John Baldwin, who later became Professor of Judicial Administration and Dean of the Faculty of Law at Birmingham University, and Allison Morris who later returned to the staff of the Institute for many years, before moving to New Zealand in the early 1990s. There she became Director and Professor of Criminology at Wellington University, and a leading researcher on Family Group Conferencing (New Zealand's distinctive version of restorative justice), as a result of which she was elected to a Fellowship of the Royal Society of New Zealand.

Allison Morris was one of the British students who benefited from the so-called 'Cambridge-Columbia Scheme', financed by the Ford Foundation, which for four years enabled a few Cambridge students to take the LLM at Columbia Law School, and Columbia students to take the Cambridge Diploma. This brought to the Institute an interesting influx of American lawyers, most of whom went on to successful legal careers in New York. One Columbia student, however, changed direction and became an academic criminologist; he is Paul Brantingham,

Rosa del Olmo, the eminent Venezuelan criminologist, who was a student on the first postgraduate course.

now a professor at Simon Fraser University, Vancouver, and a distinguished specialist in the field of environmental criminology.

Naturally, British criminology has benefited greatly from the postgraduate course. For example, one early student was the radical criminologist Ian Taylor, celebrated co-author of *The New Criminology* (Taylor, Walton and Young 1973) who worked at Carleton University (Ottawa), Sheffield and Salford Universities before becoming, for a tragically brief period, Principal of van Mildert College, University of Durham prior to his early death from cancer. In the 1970s, Michael Levi, after his Cambridge Diploma year, went on to do a PhD at Southampton. Now a distinguished academic at Cardiff University, his name is synonymous with 'white-collar crime' and the financial aspects of organised crime, fields in which he is widely acknowledged as the UK's leading expert. Joanna Shapland, now Professor and Director of the Criminology Centre at Sheffield University, has carried out a series of rigorous studies in criminal justice, most recently in the field of restorative justice; she has also on several occasions served the Institute as an External Examiner. North of the Border, Jacqueline (Jackie) Tombs has been an excellent ambassador for the Institute, first in the Research Unit of the then Scottish Office in Edinburgh, and now as a professor at Glasgow Caledonian University.

As in the early days, however, many have taken the postgraduate course en route to a career in practical criminal justice. Among them, three who completed the course in the late 1970s may be mentioned. John Crawforth studied for the MPhil as a serving probation officer, and went on to become Chief Probation Officer in Lancashire, and since 2005, Greater Manchester. He was awarded an OBE for his contributions to the Probation Service in 2008. Edward Fitzgerald QC became a very successful criminal barrister, widely respected for his human rights work and for his work with publicly-hated figures such as Myra Hindley and one of James Bulger's killers, as well as work for the widow of Jonathan Zito (tragically killed by a man who suffered schizophrenia). Some, too, have combined the worlds of academia and practice in varying ways. Nicola Padfield (née Helme), for example is a Senior Lecturer in the Law Faculty in Cambridge, and also a part-time judge (Recorder) and an Honorary Bencher of the Middle Temple. The American Christopher Stone became first the Director of the UK office of the Vera Institute of Justice and then overall Director of the Vera Institute (1994–2004) before taking up the Daniel and Florence Guggenheim Professorship of the Practice of Criminal Justice at the Kennedy School at Harvard. In 2006, he was awarded an honorary OBE for his contributions to criminal justice reform in the UK.

Paul Wiles, Chief Scientific Adviser to the Home Office and Government Chief Social Scientist. Photo by Paul Heartfield.

Applied Criminology: Diploma and MSt Students

There were of course no graduates from the part-time Applied Criminology courses until the mid-1990s, but, because many of these students (especially the police students) already held significant posts while studying at Cambridge, there is a high proportion of subsequent senior appointments. Indeed, at the last count just under half of the 39 police forces in England were headed by Chief Constables who hold a Cambridge Applied Criminology qualification, and to these must be added two Scottish Chief Constables and three Assistant Commissioners in the Metropolitan Police. One of the Chief Constables is Julie Spence of Cambridgeshire, with whom, of course, the Institute has been able to maintain especially close links. Because the Applied Criminology programme was in its early days closely linked to the national Strategic Command Course (see chapter 3), most of these chief officers were able to complete only the one-year Diploma qualification, but one (Alex Marshall, Chief Constable of Hampshire) went on to complete the full MSt degree.

Julie Spence,
Chief Constable of
Cambridgeshire.

Two of our police alumni have been particularly influential – one in England, one in Scotland – in arguing the case for the importance of research results when considering police strategies. Peter Neyroud, former Chief Constable of Thames Valley and now the first Director of the new National Police Improvement Agency, is a tireless advocate of evidence-based policing. He was selected by the Institute as the second Radzinowicz Fellow in 2008 (see chapter 12). North of the Border, Peter Wilson, former Chief Constable of Fife, was inspired by his Cambridge Diploma experience to begin a campaign for better police research in Scotland. After extensive lobbying, he was eventually successful in persuading the Scottish Higher Education Funding Council to fund the now-thriving Scottish Institute for Policing Research on a pump-priming basis.

There have been fewer senior appointments from the penology MSt course, but among successful alumni are Alan Scott, now HM Prison Service Area Manager for the South-West; Ian Blakeman, formerly Governor of Leeds Prison and now in charge of the Prison Service's policies for young offenders and for women; Nigel Hancock, formerly Head of Safer Custody in the Prison Service; and Vicky O'Dea, who after her MSt course left the Prison Service to join the private company Serco, and after a period as Director of Ashfield Prison now holds a senior management position with the company. These are all prison students; probation students joined the course at a later date, and in later years there will certainly be successes to report for them also.

The Senior Course

Unlike all those mentioned above, those who took the Senior Course were never registered students of the University of Cambridge. The Institute is nevertheless proud to have served them in what was, in most years, considered to be an overwhelmingly successful experience of study. Among the most distinguished alumni from this group are Sir Paul Condon, formerly Commissioner of the Metropolitan Police, and Martin Narey, formerly Director-General of HM Prison Service and now Chief Executive of the children's charity Barnardo's.

Remarkable teachers in my Diploma year (1972–3) included Roger Hood, Richard Sparks, Donald West, David Farrington, Derick McClintock, and David Thomas, as well as visiting lecturers such as Gerry Mars (who inspired me to study white-collar crime). Fellow students – including Larry Sherman - were no slouches either. Each of the teachers represented different social science or legal approaches to crime – and the result was not necessarily an interdisciplinary synthesis; nor were the teachers themselves always on the best of terms personally! But they all succeeded well in communicating the excitement of the endeavour. I was then fortunate to have Nigel Walker as a patient and encouraging supervisor for the PhD. His limited interest in sociology of law – and mine in penal philosophy – meant that we spent a lot of supervisions playing chess! But I was never in any doubt about his intellectual and moral support. He even helped me get into print in the Criminal Law Review with an article criticising one of his own papers. (In Italy, where I now work, such temerity on the part of a student would lead to permanent exclusion from the groves of academe – if not worse). The episode which most remains in my memory (apart from the regular disappearance of the Institute's nameplate) was the time one of my fellow doctoral students was taken off by the police accused of stealing the Institute's petty cash. Almost ready to 'confess' as a result of effective deployment of the good cop/ bad cop technique, the spell was broken when he asked in despair, 'but why would I have wanted to risk my future by taking the petty cash', only to be told, 'well, we think you wanted to commit the perfect crime'!

DAVID NELKEN, DISTINGUISHED PROFESSOR OF LEGAL INSTITUTIONS AND SOCIAL CHANGE,
UNIVERSITY OF MACERATA (PhD 1972–6)

Chapter 10

United Nations of Criminology:
Visitors to the Institute

Opposite: Another favourite place of refreshment: The Anchor.

Below: Sir Lionel Fox, the Institute's first Visiting Fellow.

he United Nations currently has 192 member states. Their Headquarters in New York City has 39 stories, is 544 feet tall, and houses 8,000 staff. Compared to this giant organisation the Institute of Criminology at Cambridge is a dwarf. However, in the specialist field of criminology its role in international exchange and cooperation could be seen to be as important as that of the 'Big Brother' at the East River. The international dimension of the Institute's work is reflected in the multinational background of its staff, its large proportion of overseas students and, last but not least, in its many visiting researchers from all around the globe.

Shortly after the Institute was established, the General Board approved a proposal to allow the appointment of scholars and experts from outside Cambridge to join the Institute for fixed periods of time. These Visiting Fellows would be appointed by the Institute's Committee of Management and become members of the University for the time of their stay. Sir Leon expected that the Visiting Fellows 'would substantially add to the role of the Institute as a centre for the interchange of ideas' and 'that, in view of the growing prestige of the Institute, we had good reason to believe that we would be able to attract persons of real distinction' (Radzinowicz 1999, p. 21).

Compared to some economic or weather forecasts, Sir Leon's prediction was extremely accurate. Although the University did not provide any financial support for the travelling and accommodation expenses of the Institute's Visiting Fellows, the scheme became very successful. In the early years it was helped by the generosity of the Ford Foundation supporting Visiting Fellows from North America. However, scholars from other parts of the world (and later from North America as well) have had to find funding from their home countries or invest their own resources for their stay in Cambridge.

The seven months I spent on sabbatical at the Institute of Criminology represent one of the most exciting experiences of my professional life. The Institute is a vital center of criminology; its faculty and the regular procession of visiting scholars and lecturers provide as rich an intellectual environment as one could hope to find anywhere. College dinners at high table, Evensong at King's College Chapel, and hanging out at the Anchor Pub are memorable parts of the Cambridge experience, but most important to me are the people. I was warmly welcomed to the Institute, and I treasure the many lasting friendships that were established there.

JULIE HORNEY, UNIVERSITY OF ALBANY, USA (VISITING FELLOW)

Cambridge inspires. It inspires at countless turns with its graceful beauty - the cherry tree at Clare College in bloom, the hush of the Wren Library, King's College Chapel illuminated by the setting sun... It inspires because of all who have trod here - Newton, Watson and Crick, Russell, Byron... Come and linger. Cambridge and its Institute of Criminology do not disappoint.

DANIEL S. NAGIN, CARNEGIE MELLON UNIVERSITY, USA (VISITING FELLOW)

The Cambridge Institute of Criminology – what comes first to my mind is the charming house at West Road, with its small offices filled with piles of papers, a kind of demonstration that scientific excellence does not depend on modern structures, no matter how well deserved the new comfortable premises are. Unforgettable are the conversations with colleagues like David Farrington, Anthony Bottoms, Andrew von Hirsch, Per-Olof Wikström – and Donald West in his wonderful cottage. Without their invaluable inputs, I never would have continued the way I did. Finally, Cambridge is also the seat of the European Society of Criminology.

MARTIN KILLIAS, UNIVERSITY OF LAUSANNE, SWITZERLAND (VISITING FELLOW)

The Institute gained much from the knowledge, experience and support of the Visiting Fellows. Two early Fellows are very good examples of this. In October 1960 Sir Lionel Fox, then recently retired as Chairman of the Prison Commission of England and Wales, became the Institute's first Visiting Fellow. He contributed strongly in helping to evolve an improved scheme for the Senior Course in Criminology, but unfortunately was unable to teach on this course or the postgraduate course as planned, as he died a year later. In 1966 Manuel López-Rey came as a Visiting Fellow to the Institute. He was Chief of the Social Defence Section at the United Nations for many years, and in this role he gained an immense experience of penal and criminological issues in many countries of the world. Our Institute benefited from his wisdom and won him as a friend who came back many times, and indeed bought a house in Cambridge. He passed away in 1987, and we were deeply moved when his widow, following his wishes, presented a benefaction to the Institute (see chapter 12).

The first Visiting Fellow under the Ford Foundation scheme was Donald R. Cressey from the University of California (Santa Barbara), who stayed in Cambridge in 1961–2 and taught on the first postgraduate course. From the 1950s, he took over responsibility for updating the textbook of his teacher Edwin Sutherland, and Sutherland and Cressey's *Principles of Criminology* (1966), was one of the most influential texts in our field. His visit to Cambridge suited his cross-cultural perspective on criminology, and it led directly to the publication of a book on Sutherland's theory of differential association (see Cressey 1964). Cressey was succeeded by no less illustrious scholars from the United States: Abraham Goldstein (Yale University), Sanford Kadish (University of California at Berkeley), Richard Tyler (Federal Judge), Marvin Wolfgang (University of Pennsylvania), Peter Low (University of Virginia), and Albert Cohen (University of Connecticut).

Manuel López-Rey (1902–87), Chief of the Social Defence Section of the UN Department of Economic and Social Affairs and consultant to the UN on criminal policy. He was a Visiting Fellow of the Institute and left a benefaction in his will for a prize to be established as well as a graduate studentship.

Albert J. Reiss jr. Photo by T. Charles Erickson/ Yale University.

Marvin E. Wolfgang was a 'giant' in criminology and President of the American Society of Criminology in 1984. His books on *The Measurement of Delinquency* (with Thorsten Sellin 1964) and *Crime and Culture* (1968) were ground breaking. Even more influential was his research (with Figlio and Thornberry) on a Philadelphia birth cohort, published as *Delinquency in a Birth Cohort* (1972) and *From Boy to Man, From Birth to Crime* (1987). Wolfgang was a Visiting Fellow in the 1960s when the Cambridge Study in Delinquent Development had already started. We learned from his advice (and vice versa). Later, he was a consultant to the Institute for the group of Home Office-funded studies on violence undertaken in the early 1970s after Parliament had taken the final vote to abolish the death penalty (see chapter 1).

There is not enough space to mention all the Visiting Fellows and their contributions to the Institute in detail. Already the mere list of names reads like a 'Who's Who' of criminology (see box on pp.120–1). However, a few examples may illustrate the range of our Visiting Fellows' activities.

Len Berkowitz, who came twice to Cambridge in the 1970s, was the first of a number of leaders in aggression research. Others were Cathy Spatz Widom (Fellow in 1975) who investigated the 'cycle of violence', Albert Reiss (1981) who shaped the sociological perspective on criminal violence, and Raul Huesmann (2000) who developed a comprehensive theory of social information processing and violence. Reiss became President of the American Society of Criminology (ASC) and carried out pioneering work on evidence-based policing. He inspired one of his students at Yale, Lawrence Sherman, who has brought the mission of evidence-based policing back to Cambridge as the current Wolfson Professor of Criminology. Gilbert Geis (1976) and Julie Horney (2001) were other Presidents of the ASC who spent time with us. There were also colleagues from this side of the Atlantic such as Josine Junger-Tas (2000), Martin Killias (2002) and Hans-Jürgen Kerner (2004) who used the time in Cambridge not only for research, but also to develop the new European Society of Criminology of which all three became presidents.

I was a visitor for three months at Cambridge in 2006 and had a wonderful time intellectually and socially. Mary Gower helped me to explore the Radzinowicz Library, especially the 18th and 19th century books. The Institute is a unique mixture of a traditional bureaucratic university and a global orientation, always aiming at the top. Formal structures are not the leading principle, but people. I consolidated the collaboration between the NSCR and Cambridge and established with Friedrich Lösel the European Network of Research Institutes in Criminology (ENRIC). With P-O Wikström I had scholarly discussions, resulting in a joint research project and theory book. I enjoyed Cambridge with its famous culture, attended concerts and watched a Champions League Final together with colleagues and 40 yelling British fans in a pub. Who wants more during a visit?

GERBEN BRUINSMA, INSTITUTE FOR THE STUDY OF CRIME AND LAW ENFORCEMENT, LEIDEN, NETHERLANDS (VISITING FELLOW)

My first opportunity to visit the Institute came in spring 1995, when Professor Anthony Bottoms invited me to Cambridge as a visiting scholar from Eastern Europe. At the Institute, I learnt from Loraine Gelsthorpe, Professor David Farrington, and others. My most impressive experience of those times was studying in the old Radzinowicz library where Helen Krarup, Mary Gower, and their colleagues helped me find up-to-date literature for my study. By an unusual stroke of luck, during my stay I was the guest of Philip and Monica Spence at St Mark's Vicarage, Newnham. They looked after me and became true friends, and Philip would even illustrate almost all my subsequent books with funny drawings of criminals, security guards, police officers, etc.

My second visit to Cambridge was in 2001. Both stays at the Institute in Cambridge were and have been very important for my academic achievements and my career in the field of criminology. They inspired me to new research and new adventures in criminology, crime prevention, criminal justice and security/safety studies.

GORAZD MESKO, UNIVERSITY OF MARIBOR, SLOVENIA (VISITING SCHOLAR)

Gorazd Mesko, drawn by Philip Spence.

Because of the work of Farrington and West, Developmental Criminology has always been a key topic of our visitors' research. Rolf and Magda Loeber, Daniel Nagin and Lea Pulkkinen are examples of this great tradition. The Loebers have been regular visitors and we sometimes feel they are a part of the Institute. And indeed, other Visiting Fellows became so addicted to Cambridge and its criminology that they returned later in official posts (eg Andrew von Hirsch, Tony Bottoms, P-O. Wikström and Friedrich Lösel).

Nearly all Visiting Fellows contributed significantly to the Institute's academic and social life. They collaborated in research projects with our academic staff, wrote joint articles and books, presented their research in seminars, gave advice to staff and students, acted as examiners of PhD students, and engaged in many discussions with our staff and colleagues at their colleges. However, the Visiting Fellows also lived a Cambridge life beyond the Institute. They enjoyed the spirit of the world-famous University and its colleges, the old town, museums, libraries, churches, theatre and choirs. Many Fellows became friends with staff members. Some found a favourite pub and investigated their theories on cultural differences in that social environment. An early Fellow enjoyed cribbage in a local pub and became a member of their team in the city's inter-pub league. The team reached the final. But unfortunately this was to take place on the same evening as a formal dinner at Trinity College to which he was invited by the Institute's Director. Of course, Sir Leon was not amused when he learned that his American colleague

In 2003 I spent three months at the Cambridge Institute of Criminology. From January through March I had the opportunity to experience the unique and stimulating environment provided by the old building which housed the Institute before it moved to Sidgwick Avenue. Most appreciated were the daily conversations with researchers and the exchange on methods, theory and crime policies. All this provided for excellent working conditions allowing me to finalise a research report on Telecommunication Surveillance during my stay in Cambridge.

HANS-JÖRG ALBRECHT, MAX PLANCK INSTITUTE, FREIBURG, GERMANY (VISITING FELLOW)

preferred the cribbage game. However, in favour of our Fellow it must be said that the pub event was a rare opportunity for a field study and that research always has priority in a scientist's life!

Other Visiting Fellows were football fans, and together with staff from the Institute watched international matches in pubs. Depending on the number of pints consumed and the achievement of their favourite teams, their comments on the matches were more or less controversial, but usually showed the same high level of expertise as their criminological discussions. Some Fellows even participated in the Institute's football matches. A rumour says that the broken ankle of a certain Director was due to rough tactics by visitors. However, the real risk factors were – as often in criminology – multiple and more trivial: English rain, a slippery pitch, insufficient training and inappropriate equipment.

Rolf and Magda Loeber.

We feel very lucky to have collaborated with David Farrington for more than two decades, which brought us regularly to the Institute of Criminology. David's great interest in the Pittsburgh Youth Study helped us tremendously over the years to improve our research and publish with him on a wide range of topics. In the old West Road our tiny office next to David's was the most practical, but also probably the coldest under the uninsulated roof. However, invariably the reception by staff, faculty and students was warm and made us feel much at ease. The new building was a great improvement in terms of warmth, comfort, quality of offices, computers and computer help. The coffee room made it possible to meet people informally. We also very much enjoyed the contacts with members of the Institute, including P-O Wikström, Manuel Eisner, (now Sir) Tony Bottoms, and Friedrich Lösel, and we benefited much from discussions with students. Our 'home' accommodation in Clare Hall added to our enjoyment of our stay as did the wonderful buildings and large number of cultural activities in the town. At Cambridge we could finish several books on the Pittsburgh Youth Study, and two books resulting from US study groups which David and Rolf conducted. We would not have been able to do if we would not found such a good welcome at the Institute of Criminology and Clare Hall.

ROLF & MAGDA LOEBER, PITTSBURGH UNIVERSITY, USA (VISITING FELLOWS)

Some Fellows used their time at Cambridge not only for criminological research but for important academic contributions in other areas. Rolf and Magda Loeber are great examples of this. They usually spent the early evening hours in the University Library looking for rare Irish novels. This balance between criminology and literature enabled them to finish their *Guide to Irish Fiction* (Dublin 2006), a volume of a mere 1,600 pages that is one of the most comprehensive collections on writers from our neighbouring island.

The Visiting Fellows were and are not the only guest researchers in the Institute. We also host many visiting scholars. Some were distinguished colleagues who only had time to stay with us for a short period. Examples are Doris Layton McKenzie from the University of Maryland (USA) or David Weisburd from Hebrew University, Jerusalem (Israel) and George Mason University (USA). There is also a larger group of scholars who are in earlier stages of their career and stay for longer periods of time. They are normally supported by stipends from their home countries and work on theses or other research projects. The Institute invests substantial resources in this Visiting Scholars scheme to promote criminology worldwide. However, it is not only a one-way-process. Not infrequently, the young researchers develop long-term relationships to the Institute or come back to study on our PhD programme. The number of Visiting Scholars has considerably increased over the last few years. Since 2005 we have hosted 35 Scholars from 18 countries: Argentina, China, Germany, Israel, Italy, Japan, Kosovo, Mexico, The Netherlands, New Zealand, Slovenia, South Africa, South Korea, Spain, Switzerland, Turkey, United Kingdom, and USA. Although the new building enables us to welcome more guests than at West Road, the size of the visitors' area and staff capacity limits our hospitality.

A third group of visitors to the Institute were practitioners who came to us as Cropwood Fellows. The background of this scheme and its generous support by the Barrow Cadbury Trust has already been described in chapter 3. When the programme started in 1968, it was far ahead of its time in encouraging busy practitioners to retreat for some time from their daily routine and carry out research on a topic relevant for their work. By 2003 some 129 Cropwood Fellows had been appointed by the Institute. Funded by the Barrow Cadbury Trust, we have just finished an evaluation of this programme (van Mastrigt & Lösel 2009). The findings show that the research of the visitors covered a very broad variety of topics, ranging from prison, probation, and police organisation and personnel development over the history of the justice system, legal decision making, and crime in the media, to juvenile, sexual, female, drug-addicted, mentally-disordered and other offender groups. Many of these studies were published in scientific journals, chapters, books, government reports or professional magazines. More than two thirds of the Cropwood Fellows who could be contacted rated the scheme as 'excellent' and 30% as 'good'. Over three quarters felt that it had had an impact on their career and many observed some impact on policy. Nearly all look back to their time at Cambridge with thanks, pride and other good memories.

The Cropwood Fellows came from Britain, but they discussed their ideas with students and visitors from other countries and thus made a further contribution to the international exchange in the Institute. In particular, they brought their practical experience. This dimension is becoming even more international since we recently opened the recruitment for our part-time MSt Courses in Applied Criminology to practitioners from overseas. Many different countries – ranging from Australia to Trinidad and Tobago – have already been represented on these programmes. In 2008 the Wakefield Trust made a generous donation that enables us to give bursaries to outstanding practitioners from poorer countries. In the past, the majority of our overseas visitors came from Europe, North America, Australia, and East Asia. For various reasons,

FITZWILLIAM COLLEGE

Institute of Criminology
Dinner

Wednesday 13th September 2006

Prawn, Tomato & Cucumber Towers
with Beetroot Sauce
✦

Sirloin Steak with a pocket of Duxelled
Mushrooms in Red Wine Sauce

Lyonnaise Potatoes
Asparagus Spears
Baby Sweetcorn
✦

Tropical Fruits with
Passion Fruit M...

An Institute dinner at Fitzwilliam College, 2006.

Africa, South America, the rest of Asia and the Arabian countries were under-represented. It is our aim to reduce this gap in the Institute's mission of 'United Nations in Criminology' in time for our 75th Anniversary.

Memories of Cropwood Fellows

Memories of Fellows quoted in the Cropwood Fellowship Programme Evaluation Report (van Mastrigt and Lösel 2009)

It was a wonderful and personally extremely valuable experience for me as I had missed out on University and yet had an academically enquiring mind. Before undertaking the Cropwood, I lacked confidence academically … it was quite a life-changing experience and I shall always be grateful for having been given the opportunity.

PROBATION OFFICER, 1991 FELLOW

It helped me academically in improving my research, but that contributed to practice as well… it helped to have two months to actually sit and read and think – in the clinical world you don't get that opportunity… it was perhaps the most important opportunity given to me in my development as a forensic psychologist.

FORENSIC PSYCHOLOGIST, 1986 FELLOW

I can honestly say… that had I not enjoyed the privilege of time-out from the hurly burly of full-time work, the future of prison inspection in this country might have been very different, and dare I say, not nearly as successful.

PRISON INSPECTOR, 1995 FELLOW

Visiting Fellows to the Institute*

Sir Lionel Fox, *former Chairman of the Prison Commission of England and Wales*

Donald R. Cressey, *University of California at Santa Barbara, USA*

Abraham Goldstein, *Yale University, USA*

Sanford H. Kadish, *University of California at Berkeley, USA*

Manuel Lopez-Rey, *The United Nations*

Judge Harold R. Tyler, *Federal Judge, USA*

Marvin E. Wolfgang, *University of Pennsylvania, USA*

Peter Low, *University of Virginia, USA*

Albert K. Cohen, *University of Connecticut, USA*

Telford Taylor, *Columbia Law School, New York, USA*

Richard Myren, *School of Criminal Justice, University of Albany, USA*

Albert J. Reiss jr., *Yale University, USA*

Leonard Berkowitz, *University of Wisconsin, Madison, USA*

James Short, *Washington State University, USA*

Sheldon L. Messinger, *Center for Study of Law and Society, University of California, Berkeley, USA*

David Levine, *University of Nebraska-Lincoln, USA*

Gilbert Geis, *University of California at Irvine, USA*

Ted R. Gurr, *University of Maryland, USA*

Cathy Spatz Widom, *University of Indiana, USA*

Martin Friedland, *University of Toronto, Canada*

Hugo Bedau, *Tufts University, Massachusetts, USA*

Stanley Brodsky, *University of Alabama, USA*

Anthony Doob, *Centre of Criminology, University of Toronto, Canada*

Barbara Huber, *The Max Planck Institute for Foreign and International Criminal Law, Freiburg, Germany*

Ilene H. Nagel, *Indiana University School of Law, USA*

Tony Bottoms, *University of Sheffield, UK*

R.P. Roulston, *Sydney University, Australia*

Jerzy Jasinski, *Polish Academy of Science, Warsaw, Poland*

John Alderson, *Chief Constable of Devon and Cornwall, UK*

Maureen Cain, *The University of the West Indies, and University of Birmingham, UK*

Norman Thompson, *Forensic Pathologist, Juneau, Alaska, USA*

Jan van Rooyen, *University of Pretoria, South Africa*

Alfred Blumstein, *Carnegie Mellon University, USA*

Richard Blum, *Stanford University, USA*

Joel Eigen, *Franklin & Marshall College, Pennsylvania, USA*

Richard Ericson, *University of Toronto, Canada*

Warren Young, *Victoria University of Wellington, New Zealand*

Raymond Corrado, *Simon Fraser University, Vancouver, Canada*

William McCord, *City University of New York, USA*

Gerald Rose, *La Trobe University, Melbourne, Australia*

Simon Verdun-Jones, *Simon Fraser University, Vancouver, Canada*

Ian Taylor, *Carleton University, Ottawa, Canada*

Timothy F. Hartnagel, *University of Alberta, Edmonton, Canada*

P-O Wikström, *University of Stockholm and National Crime Prevention Council, Sweden*

Maria Los, *University of Ottawa, Canada*

Robert Ratner, *University of British Columbia, Vancouver, Canada*

David Fogel, *University of Illinois, Chicago, USA*

Richard Wright, *University of Missouri, St Louis, USA*

Andrew von Hirsch, *Rutgers University, New Jersey, USA*

Peter Raynor, *University College, Swansea, UK*

Louise Biron, *University of Montréal, Canada*

Leslie Sebba, *Hebrew University, Jerusalem, Israel*

Frederick Rivara, *University of Washington, Seattle, USA*

Richard Kinsey, *University of Edinburgh, UK*

David Rowe, *University of Arizona, Tucson, USA*

Leslie T. Wilkins, *State University of New York at Albany, USA*

Richard Green, *State University of New York at Stony Brook, USA*

Richard Singer, *Rutgers School of Law, New Jersey, USA*

Andreas Kapardis, *La Trobe University, Australia and University of Cyprus*

Kenneth Polk, *University of Melbourne, Australia*

Christine Alder, *University of Melbourne, Australia*

Keith Bottomley, *University of Hull, UK*

Allison Morris, *Victoria University of Wellington, New Zealand*

Michael Churgin, *School of Law, University of Texas at Austin, USA*

L. Rowell Huesmann, *University of Michigan, USA*

Rolf Loeber, *Pittsburgh University, USA*

Josine Junger-Tas, *Ministry of Justice, The Netherlands*

Martin Killias, *University of Lausanne, Switzerland*

Julie Horney, *University of Albany, USA*

Friedrich Lösel, *University of Erlangen-Nuremberg, Germany*

Douglas Husak, *Rutgers University, New Jersey, USA*

Kevin Reitz, *University of Colorado, USA*

Hans-Jörg Albrecht, *Max-Planck Institute, Freiburg, Germany*

Daniel Nagin, *Carnegie Mellon University, USA*

Jean-Paul Brodeur, *University of Montreal, Canada*

Candace Kruttschnitt, *Department of Sociology, University of Minnesota, USA*

Bob Crutchfield, *University of Washington, USA*

Hans-Jürgen Kerner, *University of Tübingen, Germany*

Kathleen Daly, *Griffith University, Australia*

Roxanne Lieb, *Director, Washington State Institute for Public Policy, USA*

Tapio Lappi Seppälä, *National Research Institute of Legal Policy, Finland*

Gerben Bruinsma, *Institute for the Study of Crime and Law Enforcement, Leiden, Netherlands*

Richard Harding, *Inspector of Custodial Services, Western Australia*

Brandon Welsh, *University of Massachusetts, USA*

Magda Loeber, *Pittsburgh University, USA*

Lea Pulkkinen, *University of Jyväskylä, Finland*

Andrew Simester, *University of Singapore*

John Tasioulas, *University of Oxford*

Peter Carrington, *University of Waterloo, Canada*

Joanna Shapland, *Sheffield University, UK*

Ronald Francis, *Victoria University, Australia*

* In approximate temporal sequence; repeat visitors listed only once. Pictures of three recent Fellows are shown below.

Julie Horney.

Hans-Jörg Albrecht.

Gerben Bruinsma.

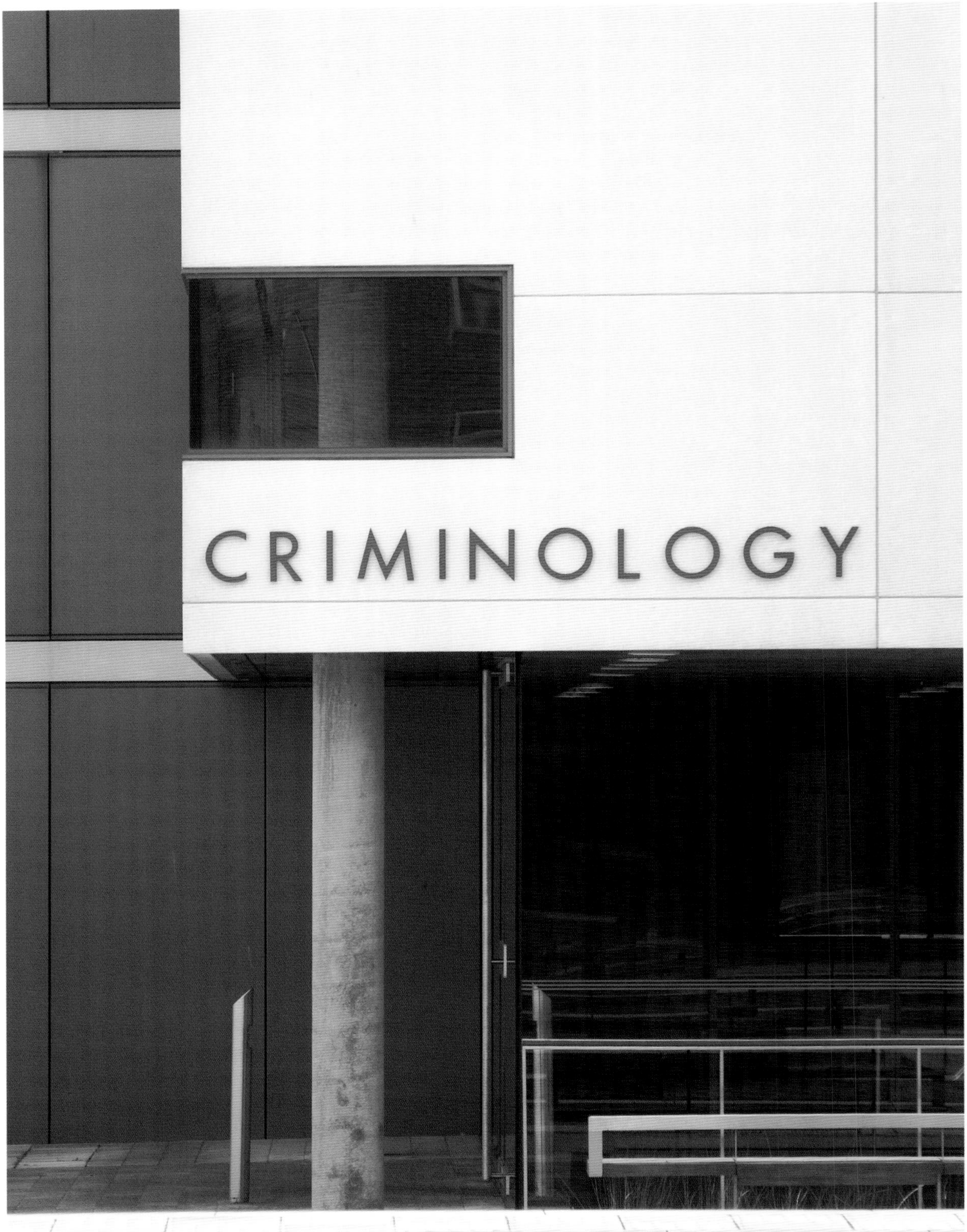
CRIMINOLOGY

Chapter 11

A Permanent Home: The New Building

A remarkable event occurred in 1984, in the first month of the Directorship of Anthony Bottoms. Over the course of a quarter of a century, the University had come to overlook the fact that, back in 1960, it had carefully put aside part of the original Wolfson Foundation endowment to create the nucleus of a Building Fund for the Institute. The money was still there, buried deep in the accounts, but neither Nigel Walker nor Donald West, as Directors, had been made aware of this fact. The information was, however, serendipitously rediscovered by a University official who had been asked to brief Tony Bottoms on his arrival in Cambridge; and, of course, the original sum had grown substantially during the period that it had lain among the University's invested funds.

Moving towards a new building was, however, far from straightforward. An initial issue concerned the accommodation needs of the Law Faculty. Traditionally in Cambridge the academic staff of most of the arts and social sciences faculties had worked from their college rooms, with only a tiny administrative office for faculty administrative staff. By the mid-1980s, several such faculties (such as Economics, Modern Languages, Philosophy and History) had broken with this pattern, and had moved to dedicated buildings on the Sidgwick Site; but Law had not. It was decided by the General Board that the time had come to change this situation, and that the Law Faculty should have a building on the Sidgwick Site; it was further decided that such a building should include both Law and Criminology. An architectural competition was held on this basis, and the firm headed by Sir Norman Foster (now Lord Foster) was appointed as project architects. A planning application was made for a joint building, but this was rejected by the Cambridge City planning authorities as inappropriately configured on the site. To remedy this, the University decided, in consultation with the architects, to separate the building projects for Law and Criminology, and Fosters proceeded to build a stand-alone Law Faculty. While the Institute's staff were glad to see our legal colleagues occupy a fine new building, it was frustrating that plans for a Criminology building were once again at square one.

There followed further delays for various reasons, and then a fresh complication. The University decided that the Sidgwick Site was in danger of becoming too uncoordinated, and that a fresh look at the masterplan for the site was necessary. There was, of course, a strong case for this approach, but the criminologists were nevertheless concerned. It was now the mid-1990s, and not for the first time the Institute found it necessary to draw the University's attention to the Wolfson Foundation's explicit statement in 1960 that its major initial grant was made on the understanding that 'suitable and permanent accommodation would be provided by the University'.

By the time that Anthony Bottoms resigned as Director in 1998, it was virtually certain that a new building would become a reality, largely because of the impetus provided by the General Board's formal review of the Institute (see chapter 1) but also because generous further funding had been promised, for example by Cambridge University Press in relation to the library element of the proposed building. However, the financial package was not yet finalised, and no practical steps had yet been taken. As noted in chapter 1, it was Michael Tonry's major achievement, in his five years as Director, to negotiate the final financial package and then to work with the architects (Allies and Morrison) to succeed at last in making the new building a reality. Interestingly, the sum set aside from the Wolfson Foundation's initial grant, carefully invested and nurtured for over 40 years, met approximately one-third of the cost of the Institute's new home.

The site of the new building during the archaeological excavations, showing the post holes of the Anglo-Saxon buildings.

Archaeological work in advance of the new building was undertaken in 2002. The most significant find on the footprint of the new building was a group of structures and pits forming a settlement of the early Anglo-Saxon period. The most important of the five structures consisted of 41 post-holes arranged in a rectangular pattern and making up the plan of an earth-fast post-hole timber building with a floor area of about 50m². Although there was no evidence of a hearth in this building, two later structures and several small pits yielded animal bones and shards of Anglo-Saxon pottery. An Anglo-Saxon burial ground had previously been found under the new Garden Hostel for King's College just across West Road, but the new Criminology building sits on top of perhaps the earliest known Anglo-Saxon domestic settlement in Cambridge. A full account of the excavation has been published in the *Proceedings of the Cambridge Antiquarian Society* (Dodwell, Lucy and Tipper 2004).

The new building was formally opened on 11 May 2005 by Lord Woolf, then the Lord Chief Justice of England and Wales, with the Vice-Chancellor of the University, Professor Alison Richard, presiding. It was a very happy occasion, and, for the Institute, the culmination of the long quest to achieve the Wolfson Foundation's requested 'suitable and permanent' accommodation (though in this context 'suitable' is definitely a piece of English understatement – the building is truly excellent). It was very good to be able to welcome the Director of the Wolfson Foundation, Dr Victoria Harrison, to the opening ceremony. A specially-made plaque in the Entrance Foyer of the building stands as a permanent reminder of the occasion.

Happily, too, in the week that the building was opened there were several other reminders of the Institute's beginnings. Lord Woolf himself had been elected as the Institute's first Radzinowicz Fellow, under a benefaction in Sir Leon's will (see chapter 12), and on the day after the opening of the building he delivered the first Radzinowicz Lecture, on the topic 'Making sense of sentencing' (see Woolf 2008). Lord Woolf's acceptance of the role of Radzinowicz Fellow was greatly appreciated by the Institute, particularly as he had contributed the Foreword to Sir Leon's last book, *Adventures in Criminology* (Radzinowicz 1999). Very fittingly, too, during his stay in Cambridge that week Lord Woolf occupied the former Judges' Lodgings in Trinity College, the college of which Leon Radzinowicz was for half a century a Fellow, and of which Lord Butler, whose initiative led to the foundation of the Institute (see chapter 1) was a former Master.

Shaping the design of the new Institute of Criminology – *Jenny Lovell*

Allies and Morrison were asked to masterplan the Sidgwick Site as a whole prior to being commissioned to design the buildings for the Faculty of English and the Institute of Criminology. The site had been developed in a piecemeal fashion over the last part of the 20th century and consequently lacked a clear identity or direction. Very early on, the then Director of Environment and Planning at Cambridge City Council, Peter Studdert walked the site with members of Estate Management and Building Service (EMBS) and Allies and Morrison – myself included. There was some concern on the part of the Planning Department that the site that was being considered for Criminology, adjacent to Law, was too small to 'take a building'. We (Allies and Morrison) actually felt that a building along that east boundary of the site would help to enclose a new court space linked to the Raised Faulty Building court, and give a clear presence to Criminology for their first purpose-built facility.

A number of architectural references were drawn upon in the early design discussions for the building and Professor Andrew von Hirsch played an active role in those discussions of the design, beyond the purely pragmatic needs of the Institute. Carlo Scarpa's work, specifically at Brion Vega, was considered (and greatly respected) in overall form and detail. The work's ability to elegantly, poignantly and timelessly 'stitch' together the old and new was an initial precedent. Scarpa's projects often focus on the detail of thresholds and interstitial spaces to create new space and this is very much how the Institute building was discussed with the Planning Department – not as a new building insertion per se, but as a means by which to connect and help redefine both the existing site and new space identified in the masterplan scheme, as well as to give identity to the relatively new discipline of Criminology.

Other precedents included seminal 20th-century architects such as Alvar Aalto and Arne Jacobsen, Scandinavian architects whose work is anchored in a strong moral humanist ethos. It was felt that the new building would have to be a 'quiet' and honest one – specifically in terms of its confined site and varied stylistic adjacencies. It had to mark its presence, but could not afford to be overstated within its context. It has both individual and civic duties.

Another influence in the early design of the building was that of the sculptor Donald Judd. His *Untitled 1986* wall piece is a complex order of rhythmical divisions with the sense of movement articulated through the action of the viewer. We considered in some detail how the reading of the building façade would change as you approached either from the north (main entry) or south (the Raised Faculty Building and Sidgwick Avenue) – the perception of the depth of the building surface changes as you move through space. As you approach the entry pavilion, the white concrete window reveals come into view, activating the depth of the facade. This concept is also reflected in the landscape design (by J & L Gibbons, landscape architects) with a 'random' planting of Himalayan Birch trees (*betula utilis jacquemontii* – tagged individually at

The architects, Jenny Lovell and Nicholas Champkins (right) at the formal opening in May 2005.

a nursery near Hamburg a year before being planted on site), their straight white trunks echoing the crisp white concrete panels – like citizens gathering in the court!

In May 2005 we joined many in celebrating the opening of the Institute of Criminology's new building by Lord Woolf. As we toured the building we came to sit at the boardroom table, above the entry and overlooking the landscaped court. Peter Studdert was there too and exclaimed that the room was possibly one of the best meeting spaces in Cambridge – affirmation of Allies and Morrison's initial vision for the siting and design of the Institute as part of its rich and complex context.

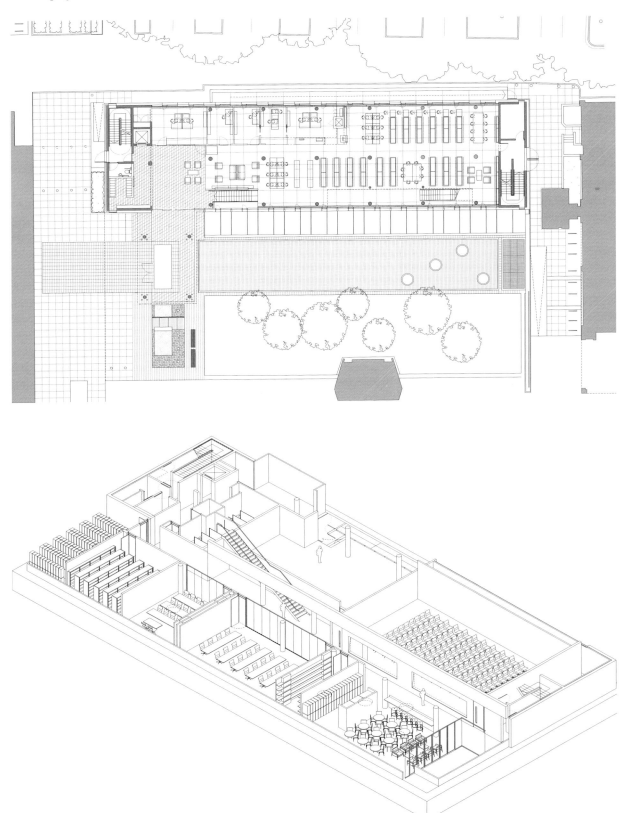

Opposite: Ground floor plan and elevation of the new building by Allies and Morrison.

The construction of the new Institute building – *Nicholas Champkins*

The new Institute of Criminology is situated to the east of the listed Raised Faculty Building. To the south, it is bounded by the Lecture Block, the first of the academic facilities by Casson Conder Architects, completed in 1959. The Faculty of Law (Foster and Partners 1995) is immediately to north of the Institute. The approach taken grew from studying Casson Conder's original vision for the Sidgwick Site which was a modern reinterpretation of the historic collegiate form where fluid, non-hierarchical public spaces replaced enclosed private courtyards. The project followed Casson Conder's belief that the public realm between buildings is as important as the more private spaces they serve. The building's entry is located off a new pedestrian axis running east from the Faculties of Divinity and History creating a new enclosed garden court to the east of the Raised Faculty Building. The primary uses of the building are to provide teaching, office and research space for the staff and postgraduate student body and to house the Institute's research library, one of the foremost criminology libraries in the world.

The building's simple rectangular plan is enlivened on the north-east corner by a projecting entrance pavilion which also contains on its upper floors the Institute's main meeting room and staff room. While sharing the same material vocabulary as the body of the building – pre-cast concrete and dark grey anodised aluminium – the pavilion breaks out of the systematic repetition of the main elevations to make a more specific response to its location.

The façade of the main building is composed of fixed full-height windows alternating with vertical panels of louvres. Behind these are shutters which can be opened to provide natural ventilation to individual office spaces. The simple rhythm of the façade is constant throughout the length of the building but adjusts in response to the presence of the library where more glass, and shading, is introduced. The insertion of a metal plate as a lining to the north – but not the south – facing reveals the concrete panels, offers a different reading of the building depending on the direction from which it is approached.

Our brief determined the following configuration. Internally the four floors of accommodation house a variety of research, administrative and library spaces. These are connected via open staircases providing informal connections between different floor levels. The library is identified as the 'heart' of the Institute, and as such it has been located at ground and first floor levels, between the larger teaching spaces at basement level, and research and office space on the second and third levels. At basement level, where the main teaching rooms and some social space are accommodated, the working areas extend under the courtyard. Hence, four circular roof lights punctuate the landscape to allow daylight into the interior, while a single line of roof glazing lights the main circulation route that runs parallel to the façade.

A successful building often acknowledges subtly how it might serve future needs, even those not yet apparent. An important component of the brief was to ensure that the building could cope with change as the users and their requirements alter. To achieve this, the building is designed to maximise the 'flexibility' of the internal arrangement. In an approach that had much in common with commercial office development, the façade and internal layout allows for internal walls to be erected every 1500mm. This strategy relies upon careful consideration of all aspects of the design that will affect occupant use and the building operation over time, for example, ventilation and heating systems.

The formal opening of the building by Lord Woolf, seated on the commemorative plaque, with (l to r) Professor Alison Richard, the Vice Chancellor, Sir Anthony Bottoms, Professor Michael Tonry and Professor James Crawford, Chairman of the Faculty of Law. Photo by Phil Mynott.

TELEPHONE
FREMANTLE 8552· 3. IX· 65·

100, COLEHERNE COURT,
OLD BROMPTON ROAD,
S.W.5.

Dear Dr Radzinowicz

I have long been an admirer of your wonderful work, both as the author of the History of English Criminal Law & in the establishment of the Institute of Criminology.

Edward Gibbon Wakefield was my great, great uncle & you yourself have drawn attention to his great interest in the plight of criminals in your great history.

the object of attracting money from other sources —

Would you let me know what you think of all this?

Yours sincerely

Priscilla William

The original letter written in 1965 by Mrs Mitchell, then Priscilla Williams, to Leon Radzinowicz, introducing herself and offering to make a donation to the Institute.

- the residue of the Clarke Hall Trust, made available to the Institute of Criminology in the 1960s for probation-related activities; the Trust was originally established in the 1930s in memory of Sir William Clarke Hall, a Metropolitan Magistrate and co-author of *Clarke Hall and Morrison on Children*;
- various small gifts from individuals, usually to augment the acquisition funds of the Radzinowicz Library, for example a gift made in memory of MPhil student Stephen Lelewer, and a gift made by the father of Baron Boulos, a prospective MPhil student who was tragically killed in a road accident before he could take up his place;
- various gifts made through the American Friends of Cambridge University.

The Institute is indeed fortunate to have been the recipient of such gifts. As we look back over 50 years, we are profoundly grateful for such magnificent support.

Sometimes, however, necessary and valuable support comes in non-financial forms. That was particularly true in the early days of the Institute, when the precarious new green shoots needed careful nurture, and also in its middle period, when there was sometimes opposition to encounter. A truly vital source of support at these times has been the Institute's Committee of Management. The first Chair of this Committee was the then President of Queens' College, subsequently Vice-Chancellor of Manchester University, Sir Arthur Armitage, of whom Leon Radzinowicz wrote that his 'disinterested and always effective help' to the Institute 'exceeds all tribute that can be paid' (Radzinowicz 1998, p. 241). He was succeeded all too briefly by Lady Adrian, a noted national figure in the field of mental health and welfare, and a former member of the Home Office Departmental Committee on Children and Young Persons (the 'Ingleby Committee', 1959–60), who died suddenly in 1966 after only a short time in post. Then Professor Oliver Zangwill, a distinguished experimental psychologist, served as Chairman for an exceptionally long period of 13 years, including the significant transition from the Directorship of Leon Radzinowicz to that of Nigel Walker. As Leon Radzinowicz was later to comment, his service to the Institute in this role was 'outstanding' (Radzinowicz 1988, p. 242).

In the 1980s, the Institute's strongest supporters were two Professors of Law, Peter Stein and David Williams, who between them held the Chairmanship of the Committee of Management from 1979 to 1992. Sir David Williams later became the first Cambridge Vice-Chancellor to hold office under the new regulations for that office (which permitted a long-term tenure, rather than a short period of office by the Head of a College). In the early 1980s, Stein and Williams ensured the defeat of a move by some traditionalists within the Faculty of Law to eject the Institute from the Faculty on the grounds that the empirical studies it conducted were not 'law'. It is an interesting comment on these events that in 2010 Oxford University Press is planning to publish a 'Handbook of Empirical Legal Studies', comprising more than 40 chapters!

The pressures of academic life in recent years have led to the typical term of office of a Chair of the Committee of Management becoming shorter. But the support has been just as vital. All recent Chairs have been senior members of the Faculty of Law, and experience during this period has again reinforced the wisdom of another of Leon Radzinowicz's founding principles for the Institute, namely its location within the Faculty of Law (see chapter 1).

To all its friends and supporters, the Institute on its 50th Birthday offers a sincere and very warm vote of deep thanks.

Opposite: The Institute at night.

Chairs of the Committee of Management of the Institute

Sir Arthur Armitage	1960–1964
Lady Adrian	1965–1966
Professor Oliver Zangwill, FRS	1966–1979
Professor Peter Stein, FBA	1979–1984
Professor Sir David Williams	1985–1988
Professor Peter Stein, FBA	1988–1992
Professor Len Sealy	1992–1995
Professor John Spencer	1996–1998
Dr Roderick Munday	1998–1999
Professor A. T. H. Smith	1999–2000
Professor Sir Jack Beatson, FBA	2000–2002
Professor John Spencer	2002–2004
Professor James Crawford, FBA	2004–2006
Professor David Feldman, FBA	2006–2009
Professor David Ibbetson, FBA	2009–

Bibliography

Bennett, T. and Wright, R. (1984). *Burglars on Burglary: prevention and the offender.* Aldershot, Gower.

Bottoms, A.E. (1998). The Cambridge Institute of Criminology. *European Journal on Criminal Policy and Research*, **6**(1), 143–51.

Bottoms, A.E. (2006). Desistance, social bonds and human agency. In P.-O.H. Wikström and R.J. Sampson (eds). *The Explanation of Crime*. Cambridge, Cambridge University Press.

Bottoms, A.E. and Costello, A. (2009). Crime prevention and the understanding of repeat victimisation. In P. Knepper, J. Doak and J. Shapland (eds). *Urban Crime Prevention, Surveillance and Restorative Justice*. Baton Rouge, CRC Press.

Campbell-Holt, C. (ed.) (2008). *Sir H. Woolf: The Pursuit of Justice*. Oxford, Oxford University Press.

Cohen, S. (1981). Footprints in the sand: a further report on criminology and the sociology of deviance in Britain. In M. Fitzgerald, G. McLennan and J. Pawson (eds). *Crime and Society: readings in history and theory*. London, Routledge.

Coupe, T. and Blake, L. (2006). Daylight and darkness targeting strategies and the risks of being seen at residential burglaries. *Criminology*, 44(2), 431–64.

Cressey, D.R. (1964). *Delinquency, Crime, and Differential Association*. The Hague, M. Nijhoff.

Davis, M. (1993). Untitled review of 'Why punish?, *Law and Philosophy*, **12**(4), 395–405.

Dhami, M.K. (2001). Bailing and jailing the fast and frugal way. *Journal of Behavioral Decision Making*, **14**(2), 141–68.

Dodwell, N., Lucy, S. and Tipper, J. (2004). Anglo-Saxons on the Cambridge Backs: the Criminology site settlement and King's Garden Hostel cemetery. *Proceedings of the Cambridge Antiquarian Society*, **93**, 95–124.

Eisner, M. (2003). Long-term historical trends in violent crime, *Crime and Justice; A Review of Research*, **30**, 83–142.

Eisner, M. and Ribeaud, D. (2007). Conducting a criminological survey in a culturally diverse context. *European Journal of Criminology*, **4**(3), 271–298.

Farrington, D.P. (1988). *Cambridge Study in Delinquent Development: long term follow-up: final report to the Home Office*. Cambridge, Institute of Criminology, University of Cambridge.

Farrington, D.P. (1989). Self-reported and official offending from adolescence to adulthood. In M.W. Klein (ed.). *Cross-national Research in Self-reported Crime and Delinquency*. Dordrecht, Kluwer, 399–423.

Farrington, D.P., Coid, J.W., Harnett, L., Jolliffe, D., Soteriou, N., Turner, R. and West, D.J. (2006). *Criminal Careers Up to Age 50 and Life Success Up to Age 48: new findings from the Cambridge Study in Delinquent Development*. London, Home Office. Home Office Research Study 299. www.homeoffice.gov.uk/rds/pdfs06/hors299.pdf

Farrington, D.P., Coid, J.W. and Murray, J. (2009a). Family factors in the intergenerational transmission of offending. *Criminal Behaviour and Mental Health* **19**, 109–24.

Farrington, D.P., Coid, J.W. and West, D.J. (2009b). *The Development of Offending from Age 8 to Age 50: recent results from the Cambridge Study in Delinquent Development.* Monatsschrift fur Kriminologie und Strafrechtsreform, in press.

Farrington, D.P., Gallagher, B., Morley, L., St Ledger, R.J. and West, D.J. (1986). Unemployment, school leaving and crime. *British Journal of Criminology,* **26**, 335–56.

Farrington, D.P., Lambert, S. and West, D.J. (1998). Criminal careers of two generations of family members in the Cambridge Study in Delinquent Development. *Studies on Crime and Crime Prevention,* **7**, 85–106.

Farrington, D.P. and Pulkkinen, L. (2009) The unusualness and contribution of life span longitudinal studies of aggressive and criminal behaviour. *Aggressive Behavior,* **35**, 115–16.

Farrington, D.P. and Welsh, B. (2007). *Saving Children from a Life of Crime: early risk factors and effective interventions.* New York, Oxford University Press.

Farrington, D.P. and West, D.J. (1995) Effects of marriage, separation and children on offending by adult males. In J. Hagan (ed.). *Current Perspectives on Aging and the Life Cycle. Vol. 4: Delinquency and disrepute in the life course.* Greenwich, Connecticut: JAI Press, 249–81.

Garland, D. (1988). British criminology before 1935. *British Journal of Criminology,* **28**(2), 131–47.

Gelsthorpe, L. (1989). *Sexism and the Female Offender: an organizational analysis.* Aldershot, Gower.

Gelsthorpe, L. and Padfield, N. (eds) (2003). *Exercising Discretion; decision-making in the criminal justice system and beyond.* Cullompton, Willan.

Grounds, A. (2005). Understanding the effects of wrongful imprisonment. *Crime and Justice: A Review of Research,* **32**, 1–58.

Hawkins, K. (2002). *Law as Last Resort: prosecution decision-making in a regulatory agency.* Oxford, Oxford University Press.

Hood, R. (1966). *Homeless Borstal Boys: a study of their after-care and after conduct.* London, Bell.

Hood, R. (1992). *Race and Sentencing: a study in the Crown Court. A report for the Commission for Racial Equality.* Oxford, Clarendon Press.

Hood, R. (2001). Leon Radzinowicz 1906–1999. *Proceedings of the British Academy,* **111**, 637–55.

Hood, R. (2002). Recollections of Sir Leon Radzinowicz. In A. Bottoms and M. Tonry (eds). *Ideology, Crime and Criminal Justice: a symposium in honour of Sir Leon Radzinowicz.* Cullompton, Willan: xix–xxiii.

Hood, R.G. and Sparks, R.F. (1970). *Key Issues in Criminology.* Weidenfeld & Nicolson.

Howard, J. (1777*). The State of the Prisons in England and Wales, with preliminary observations, and an account of some foreign prisons.* Warrington, Printed by W. Eyres.

Jarvis, F.V. (1969). *Probation Officers' Manual.* London, Butterworths.

Juby, H. and Farrington, D.P. (2001) Disentangling the link between disrupted families and delinquency. *British Journal of Criminology,* **41**, 22–40.

King, R.D. (1999). The rise and rise of supermax: an American solution in search of a problem? *Punishment and Society,* **1**(2), 163–86.

Leader, D.R. (1988). *A History of the University of Cambridge, Vol 1: The University to 1546.* Cambridge, Cambridge University Press.

Leedham-Green, E.S. (1996). *A Concise History of the University of Cambridge.* Cambridge, Cambridge University Press.

Li, C.K., West, D.J. and Woodhouse, T.P. (1990). *Children's Sexual Encounters with Adults*. London, Duckworth.

Liebling, A. (1992). *Suicides in Prison*. London, Routledge.

Liebling, A. and Maruna, S. (eds) (2005). *The Effects of Imprisonment*. Cullompton, Willan.

Liebling, A. and Price, D. (2001). *The Prison Officer*. Rugby, Prison Service Journal.

Liebling, A. with Arnold, H. (2004). *Prisons and Their Moral Performance: a study of values, quality, and prison life*. Oxford, Oxford University Press.

Loeber, R. and Loeber, M. with Burnham, A.M. (2006). *A Guide to Irish Fiction, 1650 –1900*. Dublin, Four Courts.

Lösel, F. and Beelmann, A. (2003). Effects of child skills training in preventing antisocial behavior: A systematic review of randomized experiments. *The Annals of the American Academy of Poitical and Social Science*, **587**, 84–109.

Lösel, F., Bliesener, T. and Bender, D. (2007). Social information processing, experiences of aggression in social contexts, and aggressive behavior in adolescents. *Criminal Justice and Behavior*, **34**, 330–347.

Lösel, F.A. and van Mastrigt, S. (2009). *The Cropwood Fellowship Programme 1968-2003: evaluating 35 years of building bridges between research and practice: a report to the Barrow Cadbury Trust*. Cambridge, Institute of Criminology.

Lösel, F. and Schmucker, M. (2005). 'The effectiveness of treatment for sexual offenders: A comprehensive meta-analysis'. *Journal of Experimental Criminology*, **1**, 117–46.

Lösel, F., Stemmler, M., Jaursch, S. and Beelmann, A. (2009). Universal Prevention of Antisocial Development: Short and long-term effects of a child- and parent-oriented program. *Monatsschrift für Kriminologie und Strafrechtsreform*, 92, 289–308.

Martin, J. and Wilson, G. (1969). *The Police: a study in manpower*. London, Heinemann Educational.

Martin, J.P. and Webster, D. (1971). *The Social Consequences of Conviction*. London, Heinemann Educational.

McClintock, F.H. (1963). *Crimes of Violence*. London, Macmillan.

McClintock, F.H. and Avison, N.H. in collaboration with Rose, G.N.G. (1968). *Crime in England and Wales*. London, Heinemann Educational.

Mueller-Johnson, K., Toglia, M.P., Sweeney, C.D. and Ceci, S.J. (2007). The perceived credibility of older adults as witnesses and its relation to Ageism. *Behavioral Sciences & the Law*, **25**(3), 355–75.

Painter, K. and Tilley, N. (eds) (1999). *Surveillance of Public Space: CCTV, street lighting and crime prevention*. Monsey, New York, Criminal Justice Press.

Radzinowicz, L. (1948). *A History of English Criminal Law and Its Administration from 1750: Volume I. The movement for reform*. London, Stevens and Sons.

Radzinowicz, L. (1956a). *A History of English Criminal Law and Its Administration from 1750: Volume II, The clash between private initiative and public interest in the enforcement of law*. London, Stevens and Sons.

Radzinowicz, L. (1956b). *A History of English Criminal Law and Its Administration from 1750: Volume III, Cross-currents in the movement for the reform of the police*. London, Stevens and Sons.

Radzinowicz, L. (1968). *A History of English Criminal Law and Its Administration from 1750: Volume IV, Grappling for control*. London, Stevens and Sons.

Radzinowicz, L. (1988). *The Cambridge Institute of Criminology: its background and scope*. London, H.M.S.O.

Radzinowicz, L. (1998). *Adventures in Criminology*. London, Routledge.

Rawle, T. (1985). *Cambridge Architecture*. London, Trefoil Books Ltd.

Sellin, J.T. and Wolfgang, M. E. (1964). *The Measurement of Delinquency*. New York, Wiley.

Shapland, J., Atkinson, A., Atkinson, H., Dignan, J., Edwards, L., Hibbert, J., Howes, M., Johnstone, J., Robinson G. and Sorsby, A. (2008). *Does Restorative Justice Affect Reconviction? The fourth report from the evaluation of three schemes.* London, Ministry of Justice Research Series 10/08.

Sherman, L.W. (1993). Defiance, deterrence, and irrelevance: a theory of the criminal sanction. *Journal of Research in Crime and Delinquency*, **20**(4), 445–73.

Sherman, L.W. (1997). *Preventing Crime: what works, what doesn't, what's promising. A report to the United States Congress.* Washington, DC, U.S. Dept. of Justice, Office of Justice Programs.

Sherman, L.W. and Berk, R.A. (1984). The specific deterrent effects of arrest for domestic assault. *American Sociological Review*, **49**(2), 261–72.

Sherman, L.W. Gartin, P.R. and Buerger, M.E. (1989). Hot spots of predatory crime: routine activities and the criminology of place. *Criminology*, **27**(1), 27–56.

Sherman, L.W., Schmidt, J.D. and Rogan, D.P. (1992). *Policing Domestic Violence: experiments and dilemmas.* New York, Free Press.

Simester, A.P. (ed.) (2005). *Appraising Strict Liability.* Oxford, Oxford University Press

Sparks, R., Bottoms, A.E. and Hay, W. (1996). *Prisons and the Problem of Order.* Oxford, Clarendon Press.

Sparks, R.F., Genn, H.G. and Dodd, D.J. (1977). *Surveying Victims.* New York, John Wiley.

Sutherland, E.H. and Cressey, D.R. (1966*). Principles of Criminology.* Philadelphia, Lippincott.

Taylor, I.R., Walton, P. and Young, J. (1973). *The New Criminology: for a social theory of deviance.* London, Routledge and Kegan Paul.

Thomas, D.A. (1970). *Principles of Sentencing: the sentencing policy of the court of appeal criminal division.* London, Heinemann Educational.

Tonry, M. (1995). *Malign Neglect – Race, Crime and Punishment in America.* New York: Oxford University Press.

Tonry, M. (1996). *Sentencing Matters.* New York: Oxford University Press.

Tonry, M. (2004). *Punishment and Politics; evidence and emulation in the making of English crime control policy.* London: Willan.

Tonry, M. (2006). *Thinking about Crime: sense and sensibility in American penal culture.* New York: Oxford University Press.

von Hirsch, A. (1976). *Doing Justice: the choice of punishments.* New York, McGraw Hill.

von Hirsch, A. (1985). *Past or Future Crimes: deservedness and dangerousness in the sentencing of criminals.* New Brunswick, Rutgers University Press.

von Hirsch, A. (1993). *Censure and Sanctions.* Oxford, Oxford University Press.

von Hirsch, A. and Ashworth, A. (2005). *Proportionate Sentencing: exploring the principles.* Oxford, Oxford University Press.

von Hirsch, A., Garland, D. and Wakefield, A. (eds) (2000). *The Ethical and Social Perspectives on Situational Crime Prevention.* Oxford, Hart Publishing.

von Hirsch, A., Roberts, J., Bottoms, A., Roach, K. and Schiff, M. (eds) (2003). *Restorative Justice and Criminal Justice: competing or reconcilable paradigms?* Oxford, Hart Publishing.

von Hirsch, A. and Simester, A.P. (eds) (2006). *Incivilities: regulating offensive behaviour.* Oxford: Hart Publishing.

Walker, N. (1965). *Crime and Punishment in Britain: an analysis of the penal system in theory, law, and practice.* Edinburgh, Edinburgh University Press.

Walker, N. (1968). *Crime and Insanity in England.* 2 Vols. Edinburgh, Edinburgh University Press.

Walker, N. (1980). *Punishment, Danger and Stigma: the morality of criminal justice.* Oxford, Basil Blackwell.

Walker, N. (1999). The end of an old song? *New Law Journal*, **149**(6871), 64.

Walker, N. (2003). *A Man without Loyalties: a penologist's afterthoughts*. Chichester, Barry Rose.

West, D.J. (1955*). Homosexuality*. London, G. Duckworth.

West, D.J. (1963). *The Habitual Prisoner: an enquiry by the Cambridge Institute of Criminology*. New York, Macmillan.

West, D.J. (1965*). Murder Followed by Suicide: an inquiry carried out for the Institute of Criminology*. London, Heinemann.

West, D.J. (1967). *The Young Offender*. London, Duckworth.

West, D.J. (1977). *Homosexuality Re-examined*. Minneapolis, University of Minnesota Press.

West, D.J. (1985). *Sexual Victimisation: two recent researches into sex problems and their social effects*. Aldershot, Gower.

West, D.J., Roy, C. and Nichols, F.L. (1978). *Understanding Sexual Attacks: a study based upon a group of rapists undergoing psychotherapy*. London: Heinemann Educational.

Wikström, P.-O.H. (2002). *Adolescent Crime in Context: a study of gender, family social position, individual characteristics, community context, life-styles, offending and victimisation. The Peterborough Youth Study: Report to the Home Office*. Cambridge, University of Cambridge, Institute of Criminology.

Wikström, P.-O.H. (2006). Individuals, settings, and acts of crime: situational mechanisms and the explanation of crime. In P.-O.H. Wikström and R.J. Sampson (eds) in *The Explanation of Crime: context, mechanisms and development*. Cambridge, Cambridge University Press: 61–107.

Wikström, P.-O.H. cf Farrington et al. (2009b), Crime propensity, criminogenic exposure and crime involvement in early to mid adolescence. Monatsschrift für Kriminologie und Strafrechtsform forthcoming.

Wikström, P.-O.H. and Butterworth, D. (2006). *Adolescent Crime: individual differences and lifestyles*. Cullompton, Willan.

Wikström, P.-O.H. (2010, forthcoming). Situational action theory. In F. Cullen and P. Wilcox (eds). *Encyclopedia of Criminological Theory*. London: Sage Publications.

Wolfgang, M.E. (1968). *Crime and Culture: essays in honor of Thorsten Sellin*. New York, Wiley.

Wolfgang, M.E., Figlio, R.M and Sellin, T. (1972*). Delinquency in a Birth Cohort*. Chicago, University of Chicago Press

Wolfgang, M.E., Thornberry, T.P. and Figlio, R.M. (1987). *From Boy to Man, From Delinquency to Crime. Studies in Crime and Justice*. Chicago, University of Chicago Press.

Wolfson Foundation. (1960). *The Wolfson Foundation Report 1955–1960 (First Five Years)*. London, Wolfson Foundation.

Wright, R. and Decker, S.H. (1994*). Burglars on the Job: streetlife and residential break-ins*. Boston, Massachusetts, Northeastern University Press.

Wright, R.T. and Decker, S.H. (1997*). Armed Robbers in Action*. Boston, Massachusetts, Northeastern University Press.

List of Subscribers

Paul Nigel Addicott LLB (Hons)
Dr Anthony Amatrudo
Zoë Ashmore
Jun Ayukawa
John R. Bacon JP
Estella Baker
Dr Binanda Barkakaty
Ralf Bas
Martin H. Belsky
Brent D. Bergin
Tiffany Bergin
Miss Catherine Helen Bexson
Miss S.A. Blackburn
Lucinda Bowditch
Dr C.K. Breed
Andrew Bridgeford
F. Richard Bruce
Professor Dr Gerben J.N. Bruinsma,
    Director of the NSCR
Miss Valeen Calder
Monika Calyan
Kathryn M. Campbell PhD
Ian Carter
Dennis Challinger
Gary A. Chapman Esq. BS MA MPhil JD
Helen Clarke
Humphrey Cobbold
Rt Hon. Lord Justice Coghlin
Dr Patricia Connell
John Corsellis
Mrs H. Crawforth
Tom Culver
Bill Davies
Darryl T. Davies
Rev. David Dewey
Professor John L. Diamond
Cressida Dick
Eugenia Droukas
Samantha M.N. Dugas

Dr Karen Duke
Colin Dunnighan
Caroline Edwards
Andrea Egerton
Manuel P. Eisner
Tony Farley
Colin Fogarty
Gerard Forlin
Steve Fradley
Antonio Celso Fraga
Victoria Gadd
Vincent A. De Gaetano
Christine Gardiner PhD
Ioan Gealy
Loraine Gelsthorpe
Dr Henri Giller
Victoria P.L. Goh
J.E. Gormley
Mary Gower
Ronald H.J. Graham
David A. Green
Anne-Françoise Gremling
Aleksandra Gruevska
Rebecca Anne Hall
Nigel Hancock OBE MA
Dr Ben Hardy
J.D.C. Harte
Keith Hawkins
Major Michael J. Helbig
Sabrina Henze
Richard Hibbs
Albert Ho
Gareth Sherlock Y.C. Ho
Peter K. Hosking
Dr Leonie Howe
Katherine Hunter
Ivan Jankovic
Dr Richard Jones
Vanessa Jones

Dr Birthe Jorgensen
Malcolm Kane JP
Susanne Karstedt
Dr Dominic Henley Katter
Dr H.W. Klein
Christopher J. Koegl
Nobuo Komiya
Catarina Nunes Ladeira
Dawn Lake
Gaye T. Lansdell
Paul Lee
Rhodri Price Lewis QC
Professor T. Wing Lo
Professor Friedrich Lösel
Dr Nancy Loucks
Dr Samantha Lundrigan
James C.H. Ma
Demarest Lloyd Macdonald
Dr Anna Markovska
Victoria Mason (née Wright)
Daniel L. Master
Dr Sarah B. van Mastrigt
Brenda McWilliams
Fiona Meechan BA (Hons) MPhil
George Mills
David Nelken
Netherlands Institute for the Study of Crime and Law
Peter P. Newman
Patrick P. Neyen
D.J. Nicholson MA (Cantab) MSt (Cantab)
Ian O'Donnell
Dr Chip Oehme
Dr Cyril Allen Okey Okoye
James Oleson
Helena Osterdahl
J.R. Parker
Kelley Lee Parker
Alpa Parmar

Stephen J. Pitts
Dr Derek A. Pocock
Aleksandar Prazic
Peter Quinn
Stephen Ratcliffe
Sarah Joanna Reed
Neil Richards
Peter Rogers
Professor Michael W. Ross
Elaine Seekings-Norman
Joanna Shapland
Professor Lawrence Sherman
H.S. Sidhu
Dr Beatrice von Silva-Tarouca Larsen
John Skinner
John Slater
Jonathan D. Smith
Norma Susan Smith
Julie Spence OBE BEd LLB MA MBA
Kate R. Stead
Dr Heather Strang
Jonathan C. Sweet
Dr Justice Tankebe
Barry T. Taylor
James R. Thies
Jackie Curwen Tombs
Dr Stephen Tong
Craig Tuck
Dr David P. Van Buren
Peter van der Voort, NSCR Library
J.M. Wandless
Michael Wheatley
H.H. Judge Guy Whitburn QC
Mr I.J. Whiteside
Helen Wood
Naomi Young
Georgia Zara